Dear Wally

A Collection of Snarky Advice Columns and Opinionated Essays
Reprinted from the *BlueStone Press*

Wally Nichols

Acknowledgements

I'm thankful to a great many folks for their involvement in this project. I'd like to say I couldn't have done this without them, but that's not entirely true. I would still have done it because I'm mule-stubborn. But without my editor, Virginia Somma, and the keen minds of Katie Burns, Ruth Gabriel Ray, and Nicole Walker, who all worked tirelessly for little compensation other than a few belly laughs and the tinny, peddled hustle of great fame, it would have been insanely long and plagued by embarrassing grammar missteps that would reflect poorly on my 2nd grade teacher, Mrs. Watkins, who's got to be rolling in her grave already because of this run-on sentence.

Without Helen Zimmerman ("superagentlady") who has shoved (other) people up onto *The New York Times* Best Seller List, (WTF superagentlady?!?!), this would have languished at the self-publishing level.

Without the intrepid *je ne sais quoi* of Lori Childers, publisher of the area's paper of record, the *BlueStone Press* (Stone Ridge, New York), these original advice columns would never have seen the inky light of day and would never have touched, poked and irritated the community members in the first place.

It's a miracle I haven't gotten the crap kicked out of me, frankly.

Parenthesis are to be thanked (as long as we're at it), as they allow for the conversational interjections and distractions that follow our natural speech cadence, and thus allow a written voice to come alive. I use them a lot (like, A LOT). Plus, they make good smiley faces :). And, they never get thanked. Ever.

This collection is for the beach, the bathroom or the bedside table.

Yours, from a horse farm in Kerhonkson, New York, where there's no shortage of situations in need of good old-fashioned, opinionated country wisdom (or empty parenthesis to be filled),

-W

PS: I'd like to thank the Academy (cue the exit music now, I guess), my mom (who made me look up every word I ever learned and beamed when I made up my own words) and my young daughter, Hattie, who is my axis and who has unwittingly invited me to consider life with her from three feet off the ground where there's more clutter but also more clarity.

Contents

Meet Wally 3

Parenthood 9

Serious Problems 33

World Class Advice 57

Friends and Neighbors 79

In Nature 97

Traditions 113

Relationships 129

MEET WALLY

Jackass Wally

Dear Jackass Wally,

When my friends and I read your column in our dorm room, we play a game called "Beer Wally." It works like this. We read it out loud and every time you say something stupid or try to impress us with your vocabulary, we do a shot of beer. Obviously we get really drunk doing this. Here are some of the words that got us wasted last time—vituperation, sniggered, sanctimonious, erstwhile, quadratic. Oh yeah, I almost forgot sugar booger. What the hell is that? I could go on and on. Most of us go to college but we never know what the hell you are talking about. Your answers are so full of crap that it makes me want to stick a fork in my eye. Seriously, you are the perfect example of why this area sucks and that everyone under the age of 30 wants to leave. This place is nothing more than fake intellectuals like you, dirty old farmers, dirty construction workers, hippys who think their real artists, gay guys from New York with weekend houses, and ugly soccer moms. Did you ever notice how ugly everybody is around here? You probably won't even print this letter because you're probably a pussy, but we have an ACTUAL question for your next column: Why does everybody think this area is so great when it sucks?

-Awesome Bob in Rosendale

Dear Beer Bob,

How dare you insult the entire readership of the *BlueStone Press* in one discursive, snarky, hacked-up loogie? That is MY job!

For your edification: One hippy = hippy. More than one hippy = hippies. Three or more hippies = Rosendale. (Bada BING!)

Dirty old farmers grow the barley and hops that constitute the grog into which you push your punkass snout when you are playing Beer Wally (and not studying in the library?!). You sure you wanna so overtly jam the farmers?? Revenge (like beer) is a libation best served cold... And where the hell are my Beer Wally royalties?

You can probably get away with insulting hippies, if you must, as they are an insouciant bunch. We farmers, on the other hand, have backhoes and shovels and aren't afraid of putting fresh manure in its (your) proper place.

Not sure what soccer fields you are lurking around (does your probation officer know you are up to this?) but the soccer moms I see at my kid's games are smokin' hot (and that means YOU in the Subaru—you know who you are!).

"Awesome" Bob, I have to call you out on your improper use of their/they're/there. Copy editing is petty stuff and I hesitate stooping to your level (I make my fair share of mistakes), but you made it to college (presumably out of 7th grade, too?) not knowing *witch* word to use when? "Vituperation" has more letters then/than (your choice, sir!) you give it credit for. Dangle THAT preposition, for you seem above the lowly station of proper grammar use!

I think you SHOULD lead the disgruntled youth movement out of this area, single file. Gather up your Xboxes and Justin Bieber posters and leave this Hudson Valley, cat-turd sandbox! Make a parade of it! What self-respecting , upwardly mobile go-getter like yourself (with a fork sticking out of his eye) would want to hang around the stunning mountains, biking trails, summer swimming holes, dirty organic farmers, gifted musicians, writers, actors, cool coffee shops, and (eeeek!) folks with weekend houses! Best you leave the moment you finish college in 2030!

Don't worry about the rest of us you leave behind. We'll try hard to make it…

Meanwhile, here are some words for your saucy, beer-quaffing, pleasure: insolent, puerile, impudent, laggard, dolt… (You drunk yet, or should I keep going?)

Yours in the battle to eliminate idiocy,

-Wally

Got a question for our columnist or just want to vent without paying for therapy? Email him at cwn4@aol.com.

Beth and Jerry

Dear Wally,

We are weekenders accustomed to the sharp wit and crisp writing of publications such as *The New Yorker*, yet on our arrival in our Hudson Valley country home on Friday nights, tired as we are, we fight like slapping monkeys for your "advice" column in the *BlueStone Press*. I don't think in all the years of reading it, I've ever come across anything even close to advice. You are offensive, riotously funny, sentimental, outlandish, and obnoxious, sometimes in the same sentence. (Still laughing that you wrote a letter to your cat, calling her more promiscuous than a three-dollar whore. And still choked up reading your fatherly musings about your five-year-old daughter's bath time.) You seem perfectly able to prattle on regardless of the topic and I'm equal parts baffled, amused and envious. Your mind is an interesting thing. Is anything off limits? It doesn't appear so.

You do make my husband and I laugh out loud regularly, and that's no easy task. In some respects, you have a hard job because the column remains fairly local in theme. In one you signed off as Wally, PhD, suggesting you have earned a doctorate. We are both academics and protectionists of the high academic distinction that cost us countless years and money. Can you substantiate your credentials? (Institution? Year?)

Beth (and Jerry)

PS: You always have a PS. Why don't you just incorporate the afterthought into your response before sending it off?

Dear Beth,

You make me smile with the "PS" comment and, of course, where you put it!

-Wally

PS: Damn, everyone's a critic! I'm glad you guys are engaged with the column (one way or another). I love writing it and love having a platform that allows me entry into so many people's bathrooms, beach bags and bedside tables (without having to actually be there and smell them). I consider this column a gift. I receive plenty of fan mail AND plenty of hate mail. I'm gonna rip your letter in half and put one half in each pile, ok? It's nice to know, at least, that my constant drivel is getting a reaction. And, my mind is more like a superfund site!

PPS: I never said I *earned* a PhD. I believe I said I *bought* one. Online. Five years ago. (Do love me some internet!) And you can, too! Twenty-five dollars from the Universal Life Church, where I am also a five-dollar minister and thus allowed to marry my friends (and farm animals). Also allowed to slap the "Clergy" tag on the rear view mirror and park right up front at Walmart.

PPPS: I'm the first to admit that my column makes excellent fire starter and puppy cage liner. Here's some real advice: Don't take anything I write too seriously. I don't.

PPPPS: Good to know that fully grown and educated PhDs can still slap it around like monkeys!

PPPPPS: Also good to know that the plural of monkey is not monkies. Crazy English language...

PARENTHOOD

Best about Daughter

Dear Wally,

You recently became a father. What do you like most about your baby?

-JR

Dear JR,

I like the size of my baby girl's head. It's the perfect little cantaloupe. I like the smell of her head, too. It smells like organic almond oil and Burt's talc-free corn starch. It also smells like my lips. If she goes bald, it's because I've worn down a spot on the top from over-kissing it. I like seeing her nurse and then drift one eye cautiously to me as I hover over her and her mother tries to shoo me, a distracting agent, away. She's inspecting me, this baby, checking me out with tentative approval, yet mostly focused on the immediate tasks of eating and enjoying maternal comfort.

I like the way she rocks up on all fours on the bedspread and jerks back and forth to reggae when she's happy. (We call this dance the "Hootchie Momma." We will unlearn it before college). I like the way her chunky little feet poke through warm terrycloth leg holes and wiggle at the new day. And the look of complete sensory overload when we lower her into a tepid bath and she doesn't quite know if today she likes it or not. I like the way she shoves everything into her mouth, maybe because that's what I do. And the way she grabs the phone and flings it off the desk and across the room with those bionically strong fingers that look like miniature ears of corn from the Chinese restaurant. (Did she learn this from me during a recent encounter with a Verizon customer service representative? Nope. I felt like doing it but didn't.)

I like how she's startled by her own actions. Must be a curious thing to be startled by the newness of your actions… I like that

9

she can nap from 4-5pm. Or any time she damn well pleases. That's pretty neat. I like how she has a homing device in her hand that guides her to my eyeglasses no matter how dark it is, no matter if she's even looking in my direction. I like how she bops me on the nose and eagerly awaits my verbal "honk." It's a game we play and a conditioned response for us both now.

I especially like how she throws her arms around my neck already, even before she understands it'll get her anything she wants. It's one of my favorite things ever, ever in this entire world. I like how she can curl up in my arms and drift off to sleep, no matter the noise. And how she gets tired of me typing at my computer and starts demanding attention by smacking the keys. Like this: kjsdhkvhfqhoincvwjjjjjjjjjjjjjjjjjjjjjjjjjjjjjjjjjjjjjjjjj.

I like the raw ambition she has for movement. And that the energy she expends to stand upright, a goal of the highest consequence, conks her out so thoroughly. What focus! What efficiency! I like the miniaturization of fingernails, which before we clean them have the telltale signs of hard play, not hard work. I like how she squeals with unabashed delight when I lift her above my head and play airplane. The exhilaration of being suspended off the ground is almost too much for her. I also like how her laugh, which starts off sounding like a cardboard box being dragged on a barn floor, skipped two generations from my own paternal grandfather and landed in her body. I've missed it all these years since his death.

If you tickle her just right, you can get two dimples at once. And if you miss, you get a scowl. I like seeing her so happy in her mother's arms, safe and sound. I like the triangulation she has allowed our family. And the things she has taught me to do, like take smaller bites and how much fun it is to smack wooden blocks together. I even like changing her diaper because it means she'll feel better when I'm done and I'll have done my part to help ruin another landfill. I like that she's not afraid of our dogs or our horses, and instead considers them as natural as a sunny day.

I like watching her try to eat an apple, gumming it and savoring it for the brand new sharp flavor and curious texture it offers. I like that her favorite "toy" is my guitar which I play for her every day that I can. I like that she tries to eat the books we read her. I can brag and say she's a voracious consumer of literature and not be lying. I like that she and I look like we've just been in the world's most successful (and fun!) food fight after every meal I feed her.

I like that she wails for us when we hand her off to a babysitter. I like that it only lasts a moment until she realizes she's ok and there's lots to do and experience. I like that she's so young and that her sense of wonderment is pure and primal. Same with her sense of exploration and trust.

What I don't like is that that sneaky bastard Time has just sprinted out of the building with my credit card, car keys, and a snicker and I can't seem to catch up.

-Wally

PS: Thanks for asking!

Got a question that needs answering or baby's head that needs smoochin'? Contact our advice columnist at cwn4@aol.com or visit his blog www.wallynichols.com.

Flying with Toddler

Dear Wally,

Any advice for flying across the country with a toddler for the first time? I've heard (and seen) other parents' horror stories. Now it's my turn. Help!

-Beth

Dear Beth,

Ok, ok. Stay calm. I have recently crossed the country with my infant and the good news is we all survived. Got to figure that seven hours of anything, good or bad, will be over in seven hours and one minute.

We started out ok. We timed the flight so we'd be flying at night and thus our cherubic 16 month old would be sleeping. But once we got to the airport, plans tore asunder—she was on fire. Never mind the second wind. She was well into her fourth or fifth wind and racing around by the time we cleared security (annoyed maybe that she had to take off her squeaky shoes?). So many strange-smelling people and a palpable pulse of stewing international excitement only fed her energy level. It was pretty cute actually.

She quickly learned that rubbing her hands on the terminal's water fountain resulted in a panicked, five-alarm, bio-hazmat decontamination by both parents. That happened about 20 times with her and our respective joys being inversely proportional. I'm not especially germaphobic but the Newark Airport concourse water fountain is pretty much ground zero for the nastiest of the nasty, second only to its restroom. (This airport is one place I'd happily consider wearing an adult diaper.) Back-up wipes were already checked in the muthaship supply bag so we did a silent and reverent (and ultimately futile) prayer to the diaper gods to leave us be for a few hours, but that's always a gamble and the house usually wins.

At this age, exploration is everything and these little 16-month-old peckers move fast. Especially in public places. Short of putting her in a straightjacket, we had to just intercept and do damage control. Oh, and apologize for the newspapers and M&M's whipped to the floor. (This jerky, uncontrolled ambulatory phase, we're told, is temporary. I'm pretty sure the next phase will include all out sprinting and I'm not certain this 40 year old in decent shape will be able to keep up without a dart tip dipped in elephant tranquilizer and a bamboo blowgun.) Meanwhile, the thought bubbles above the passengers' heads in Alaska Airline's Flight 7 waiting area read something like this:

> "Holy crap."
> "Control your kid, damn it."
> "How were they allowed to have children?"
> "Maybe Earth will be hit by an asteroid and we won't have to sit next to them."
> "Honey, did you pack the injectable Kava Kava?"
> "Is that kid a bomb-sniffing dog in disguise?"
> "She may be all over the place but she sure is one cute kid."

They finally called the flight and we had the good sense to board very last (the idea being to minimize the passenger exposure ratio). Our plane mates avoided eye contact. We heard the exhales of relief and caught discreet high fives as we moved past them and inched toward the rear, which felt surprisingly like the banishment it was.

A small child has no idea that sitting in a bouncy seat for one third of a day will have any payoff. One can easily imagine their frustration when forced to sit in a lap beyond their allotted patience. To compound things, our snuggly "frontpack" had to be unbuckled and shoved below the seat for takeoff and landing. The reasoning, from the mouth of an equally dumbstruck flight attendant, was that the device hadn't yet been tested by the FAA for crash integrity and thus the child had to be held in our skinny, weak arms.

I suppose that slamming into the earth at 550 mph in the event of a crash might be marginally better in a parent's arms, but who cares at that point? Besides, don't we need free arms to grab our ankles so we can more easily access our rears for the famed goodbye kiss? Common (not corporate) sense says if you make a baby sit on a parent's lap in the first place, then let the baby be strapped into whatever device the parent wants.

The unfortunate soul in 25F tried to melt into the window when he saw us coming. He didn't even fake a smile. His number was up and he knew it. He must have run over a nun with his car in a past life. I tried (sometimes successfully) to block the Cheerios our daughter chucked at his head with great amusement. This trip was now all about triage and I figured a battery of small oats to the head would leave no permanent scars on this guy. I turned my focus to bigger problems, like trying to keep the three of us from getting thrown out at 35,000 feet.

Halfway through the flight, I caved and spent an hour locked in the bathroom with our daughter letting her "work it out" (read: caterwaul) until she finally fell asleep. My ears have rung less after rock concerts.

A brief quantitative summary:

> Number of wipes used: 230
> Number of friends made on flight: 2
> Number of potential friends lost on flight: all but 2
> Number of people onboard we will never see again: 158
> Amount I care, on a scale of 1-10: 0

Advice? Pack a bottle so your kid can swallow during altitude changes. Bring an extra pack of wipes. Sit near the back. Get an aisle seat. Tie a string to the Cheerio(s). The new-age cliché be damned: When it comes to air travel with an infant, it IS the destination, not the journey. Remember, seven hours and one minute and it's over! And take the hit upfront—think of the fun you'll have when you get there! Seriously, don't worry about it too much—every parent has gone through the same thing.

-Wally

Got a question for our advice columnist or just want to know what flight he will next be on so you can change your ticket? Email him at cwn4@aol.com.

Dear Wally,

What measures do you recommend I take to keep my family safe in public restrooms?

-High Anxiety in High Falls

Dear High Anxiety,

I rarely find myself aligned with the Catholic church, but on this subject I have to embrace the time-honored policy of abstinence. Specifically, one should avoid using public restrooms if possible, a notion that I guess hardly needs stating. That said, I can share a few tips that my slightly neurotic, iron-bladdered mother shared with her brood on the subject, for emergency use only. Perhaps they will be of help to your loved ones?

> 1. Jiggle the empty Gatorade jar at the kids in the back seat and say, "If you hadn't drunk it in the first place, you wouldn't need to refill it, now would you??"

> 2. "Feather the nest." As in, drape small, ripped-off sections of toilet paper (approximately 10 inches long) over every conceivable inch of the exposed public toilet seat. Make a thick lasagna that is interwoven and tight and flows over the bowl's edge like the flowering gardens of Babylon. You should be able to lift a bowling ball between any section of the mesh. Only that thickness will keep nasty germs from jumping on board your loved ones for a lifetime free ride. Never mind that you might be the reason for the high deforestation rate. Never mind that you then create a whale-choking bolus that has no chance of ever passing through anything other than an industrial stump grinder. (That problem is SO somebody else's!) Never mind the wheelchairs that are starting to queue up outside

the handicap stall you have commandeered (you'll need the elbow room and besides, you have your own handicaps—they just haven't been diagnosed). Never mind the impolite coughs from the next ten people waiting. You'll never see *them* again! Never mind any of this. A proper nest-feathering may take up to ten minutes. Remember, bowling-ball strong. Spend the time.

3. NEVER touch the handle. Ewwwwwww!?!? This is basic stuff, people. Handles were not meant to be handled. Especially by hands. As far as you are concerned, handles are to be kicked indiscriminately with the heel of your shoe. The catch, of course, is that when enough people do this, the entire toilet fixture tends to get jarred off its mounting and can be dangerous for folks with poor balance or weak thigh muscles. This is not your problem. Kick that handle like you are trying out for Manchester United. Kick as if your life depends on it. It may just…

4. Germs can travel up to 25 feet when a toilet flushes. (Do the math—with 300 million people in the US alone, there is virtually no safe place on the entire North American continent except for a small cabin in a remote corner of the Yucatan peninsula.)

5. DO NOT EVEN THINK about picking up discarded reading material and reading it. Reality check: That newspaper no longer has its virginity. That newspaper was handled by another person's hands—hands that were busy before, during or after with other tasks, know what I mean? Do you see a Purell station in that stall? *I* don't…

By the way, when you asked how to stay safe in public restrooms, I was assuming germ/microbe safe, not Senator Larry Craig safe. The rule book on *that* is still being written…

Good luck and keep the Gatorade bottles handy.

-Wally

PS: Ever at a loss for winning cocktail-party conversation? Here's some riveting trivia: The world's foremost ceramic toilet bowl design work (!?) happens in the sleepy upstate college town of Alfred, New York!! (Well, c'mon, it has to happen *somewhere...*). And, 41 percent of the people worldwide lack access to a toilet. Don't ask me how I know.

Got a question that needs answering? Ask Wally for yourself at cwn4@aol.com.

Open Letter to the PetSmart Guy

Regarding Manicotti # 1 and #2 (deceased),

Do you remember me from a few days ago? I was the guy with the cute three-year-old whose ski jump nose was pressed to the glass of the fish display in your store because there was nothing in the world she wanted more than a beta fish that she could name Manicotti. Remember how she said, "I want that one" and pointed to the one fish out of hundreds that looked drunk and listed like a floundering Carnival cruise ship that had just taken a sixty-foot rogue wave to the port side?

You scooped it out and placed it in a plastic hot-and-sour soup container for me, which may or may not have been clean. I said I didn't want to be rude, but Manicotti looked, well, wilted, uninspired, and deflated. I said there was something off—that it lacked a certain "joie-de-vivre."

You said you didn't speak French.

Then I asked if fish can puke. I've seen enough things about to throw up in my day to know this bug-eyed fish was looking ill and queuing up for something.

I wondered out loud if you guys doped 'em up after hours so they wouldn't be too hyper and either scare off potential customers or simply eat too much of your PetSmart flakey fish food. I wondered if maybe you guys warmed their bowl's water to sedate them and had inadvertently partially cooked them? (Our sixth grade math teacher would turn up the classroom heat so we'd pant and melt into compliance).

Anyway, you assured me Manicotti #1 was fine—that he was a fighter and that he would be a great starter pet. We all laughed. Remember that?

I placed my hand on your shoulder gently and whispered so my kid couldn't hear, "What do you mean by 'starter,' exactly? What am I getting into here?"

You replied, "Well, you will probably outgrow him and want to upgrade to a deluxe salt tank like this." And you ran your fingers along the fine lines of an exotic, and frightfully expensive, 3,000-gallon tank right next to it.

At that point you actually answered my question and told me beta fish can last up to four years. Four years is pretty good for a two-dollar fish with a fourteen-day guarantee. I can deal with that. Good ROI.

I, too, sometimes get lost in the time-space continuum, so I don't fault you, PetSmart guy. But twenty minutes after we left the store, Manicotti #1 was belly up. That's not exactly four years. Actually, not even close. My daughter told me from her car seat that I needed to put new batteries in the fish because it "wasn't working" anymore.

I spun around and went back in to pick up Manicotti #2 hoping she would not even notice the passing of her new BFF. I guess you had already been promoted to regional manager because you were gone.

Funny thing is, Manicotti #2 didn't make it much further than Manicotti #1.

Did you guys have a Gamma ray blaster in the PetSmart parking lot that nukes only fish?

Now, I know my car can be a toxic environment, especially after a long hard winter, but other things have gotten into it and lived at least twenty minutes, including myself, my family, a couple of dogs, and a rabid, three-pawed raccoon I was illegally transporting over state lines to some jerk in New Jersey who deserved it. In short, none of us, including Manicotti #1 or #2, have died in my car due to "environmental" issues.

Beta fish, you told me, are also called Chinese "fighting" fish, and I'll put that in quotes. Where the hell was the fight? Manicotti #1 and #2 just rolled over and floated to the top. They gave up! I get that they are only two dollars, but really??

You guys took back dead and bloated Manicotti #1, which was decent. Dead Manicotti #2 was my problem because I couldn't spend the rest of the day going back to Kingston. And I didn't want to chuck him in my freezer to preserve him for my eventual return to your refund department, so I dumped it (him? her? How the heck do you check their gender?) in the compost bucket (not the toilet) and resolutely wiped my hands. So much for fish.

But my child was watching and was duly horrified by the senseless loss of the day. I had to get into the whole life/death cycle with her a few years before I wanted to.

Poor kid, she probably wondered just how well she'll fare with a parent unable to keep a fish alive for more than twenty minutes.

Maybe I'll just buy her a bag of Pepperidge Farm cheddar goldfish. Can't kill those can we??

-Wally

Got a question for our advice columnist or just need someone to fish-sit? Contact him at cwn4@aol.com.

Reflections in the (Bath) Water

Daughter,

You swing a single, chunky, naked leg over the side of the claw foot tub, and before even dipping a toe into the water, declare with unyielding urgency (and tearing eyes), that it is way too cold, or way too hot. The negotiations and stall tactics for avoiding the dreaded hair wash, which you have trotted out all day, have been almost completely exhausted. ("After breakfast, Poppa." "No, after lunch." "No, no, no, after playing." "No, how about after dinner?" And the most crafty parent-slayer of all, "After a book!") Ultimately this day, like all of them and like all the slippery years, has gotten out from under us.

The bathroom door is now closed, and with that goes your only chance of escape—through my legs like a greased piglet, streaking and squealing "jail break" victoriously, charging through the house, arms in the air. It happens a lot and it's a sight for sore eyes! If you weren't so darn naked, I'd post it on YouTube for the world to enjoy.

Except for the thermal objection bleated loudly enough for Child Protective Services to hear, which will buy you two extra seconds while I triple-check the tepidity of the water, the jig is up. It is tub time for you, my little four-year-old sweetheart. Nice try, though. It's time for you to toss toys in the water like a mad chef cooking up a fantastic stew by using everything in the kitchen. And it's time to face the music.

The fact that you need cleaning in the first place is a good thing, though you won't see it this way for years. Life on a farm can be dirty business. This hand-off of day to the night's protective faeries is a good intersection for reflection.

You woke me up with a terrific kick to the temple at 7am after sneaking into my bed when I was fast asleep. After that abrupt reveille, we had scrambled eggs fresh from your favorite hen "Bob Marley," as well as raspberry yogurt, some good portion of which is still on your clothes, crumpled as they are now in a heap on the bathroom floor.

After breakfast, we suited up and smashed through some driveway puddles filled with last night's rain showers on our way to the barn. We brushed and tacked up Holy Mac, the miniature pony you got from your adoring grandma. The one you generously share with other young riders. I snapped the chinstrap on your helmet together because your fingers aren't yet strong enough to do it. After you climbed the mounting block by yourself and got on, I led you down the driveway and through the fields at the walk, a speed that somehow doesn't feel slow enough.

You fought fiercely to get me to let go of the lead rope so you could ride all by yourself. It didn't sit well with you when I objected, though I'll always say it can't hurt to ask, and I admire your moxie. To say this was an apt metaphor for all aspects of your burgeoning independence is an understatement. I see equal parts of your mother and me in your headstrong desires, and I honor that, albeit from the other end of a tightly clenched three-foot rope that I will someday have to relinquish.

You see, it's impossible to not want to be your friend. You are smart, funny, kind, passionate, articulate, strong-willed, athletic, clever, cute, sensitive, and important.

You are also just four.

I want to gently nudge you away from life's steep edges, yet still let you see what's on the other side so you can extrapolate and protect yourself when I'm not there to yank you back if you've gone too far. I am here now, but I won't be forever.

I also want to make sure you get a keen sense of right and wrong, as I see them anyway, and that you get the tools to articulate your thoughts and creativity and frustrations. I want to help you cultivate a desire to learn far beyond what they teach you in school. I want to make sure you treat others and yourself with respect. And that you learn to not fear fear or even fear change. I want to make sure that you slow down once in a while in this world you are rushed through. A bath is a good place to do that.

For a while anyway, I police what goes into your mouth, making sure the plastic toy parts, dog medications, boogers and Twinkies don't, but the broccoli spears, birthday cakes and cups of water do. It's my job to try to make tooth brushing fun (a near impossible task). And when I fail at that, it's still my job to make sure those teeth get brushed.

It's also my job and pleasure to make sure we get outside and get nice and dirty (sometimes *really* dirty) while seeking adventure, whether it's in a playdate or getting right down in the dirt with you. It's also my job to make sure after all that, and before I tuck you into bed with your assorted stuffed dolls and monkeys, you get clean. That includes getting behind the ears and under the fingernails, just as was done to me at your age. Oh, and we can't forget your hair.

None of this feels like work to me, by the way, though sometimes it is at odds with "friendship," at least in some sense. In fact, I have a fantastic time with all of these "jobs" but they won't take a back seat to being your friend, or I will have lost the plot. Later in your life, ideally, friends that you get to choose (not just kids your age whose cool parents I like hanging out with) will help you stay your course of good decision making and offer correction and support if needed while hopefully giggling and getting into mischief and helping you push back against whatever is in your way and or just push back against whatever needs it. I hope I get to be one of these friends. But for now, your friends get a pass on the gritty stuff. That's where I come in. And that's why your tears of protest, and cuteness, won't work on me and get you out of tonight's hair wash any more than they worked on the last one, or than they will on the next one.

But I'll still do my best to make it fun and minimize the tears.

While you push a few rubber duckies through the bubbles and try to distract me from remembering the task at hand, I sit on the nearby toilet's closed lid and pick up my guitar. I've been singing to you for years now. In fact, when I'm on key (hallelujah!) and you are not splashing me with water (double hallelujah), it probably is somewhat soothing. It is for me and you may someday even have bits of memories from this time of me and you singing during your bath. You know all the words to our favorite tunes and I love hearing them in your sing-songy, little-girl voice as you play with articulation, pitch and tonality.

When you are done crashing rubber duckies into each other, and I move ominously closer with the shampoo, a look of simultaneous terror and resolve washes over you. You are petrified but you know you are safe. It's an interesting paradox. I'm careful to avoid getting water in your eyes, and especially careful about soap, but there still is Almighty wailing. My oh my!

I run my hands through your hair, pushing the soap away from your eyes and in so doing, massage your scalp. Someday I hope you will be able to give your own child a hair wash. It's a magical feeling. If you read this as a parent, you will probably be amazed at how some things just don't change over the years.

I will then scoop you out of the tub with a warm, dry towel and give you the choice of being wrapped like a cheese burrito or a bean burrito. You will say cheese, and then immediately change your mind to bean, as if the world depends on it. No matter. Same yummy ingredients.

Then I will turn on the hair dryer and you will shriek loud enough for Child Protective Services (again!!) to hear that it's too cold, or too hot. You will yank it from my hands with righteous indignation and do it yourself, leaving me only to brush your hair, a task that feels as primal and parent/child connecting as any in the animal kingdom.

There will be a day soon when it will no longer be cool for dad to brush your hair, or even be in the bathroom when it's tub time. And when that happens, the chapter closes forever. It's no wonder I love bath time with an amplitude that perfectly mirrors your dislike of it.

So look at me with whatever puppy dog eyes you want, but you are not getting out of it. Not this year!

I love you. And your squeaky clean hair!

(And remember that you aren't necessarily the only one with tears in your eyes at bath time.)

-Me

A Good Book

Dear Wally,

Read any good books lately?

-Marcy (Stone Ridge)

Dear Marcy,

Like many caught up in the hurly-burly of life, I long to have the quiet time to drop into a red velvet smoking jacket and revisit the classics. That said, and being the parent of a toddler, my "A" list is topped with an efficient, portable stand-out. An inflatable life donut in a sea of sinking mediocrity, this book works for all ages. Let's meet the soon-to-be-classic, intensely popular, *Where Is Baby's Belly Button?* by Karen Katz.

This future member of the literary canon's title is more a rhetorical question than a literal one. In this gripping, intensely short work, a solitary child (our most innocent, fragile member of society and the one the author suggests needs the most protection and nurturing from proverbial village it takes to raise him/her, errrr, mankind?) endures the frustration of ignorance, the heartbreak of adult betrayal, the exhaustion of exploration, the sweet nectar of self-discovery, and finally the elation of vindication. The narrative turns on themes of redemption, awareness, modesty and perseverance that are as delicately intonated and intricate as a honeybee's waxy knees.

It's quite a ride, this tale—one your child may seem to *never* tire of hearing. And understandably... Big questions get answered and we as readers are able to leave the experience with a sense of fulfillment, satisfaction, and unslakable thirst to reread (and reread again) for deeper meaning. (It's like peeling an onion, though every layer still tastes like onion.) Dickens himself chronicled the human condition as deftly in but two of his works (I can't remember which two) and comparatively, his attempts mostly leave one feeling like they have just eaten a dirt sandwich. Nutritional maybe at some elemental level, but hardly worth the prodigious effort. Yet Dickens and Katz will be shelf-mates on the great mantle of posterity, mark my words.

In the book's ostensible plot, "baby" (yours?) can't find her belly button. Upon lifting a small flap of interactive cardboard masquerading as a shirt, the belly button is revealed. The "ah ha" moment you don't expect pays off every time. Your baby laughs, you laugh, and all feels right in the universe.

But grab a hankie and a headlamp. Venture beneath that cardboard flap and you get to the kernel of what this author is really saying. To wit, things in this life are not always so obvious. If one wants to know where a belly button is, one has to put in the work. One needs to feel the burn of curiosity, the hobble of despair, else nothing in life will have genuine meaning or value. Life is a zero-sum game, she suggests. To use a tired cliché, you can't know good unless you have known bad. What is the elective exhilaration of ice cream without the sour gum rub of mandated Brussel sprouts? Et cetera, et cetera.

For Katz, this is a lesson that can't be taught soon enough. (For ages one and up!) The author, rightly so, hammers the point home early by posing the question other ways. Where is baby's nose? Where are baby's feet? Where is baby's head? And so on (and so on) (and so on).

If you fall for the clever trap that this is just about a banal belly button romp, you need to get back to your literary analysis basics. The revered Algerian semiotic deconstructionist philosopher Derrida, for one, has produced much fontanel-bulging information on symbols (such as belly buttons) if you dare to go there. But beware, take on this literary avoirdupois and it might be a long trip back to the surface!

Button serves it up fresh in seven compact pages. Each page is made of water- (and puke-) resistant cardboard, brightly illustrated and replete with a tenacious, anti-rip hinge mechanism. I personally have read it at least 4,000 times and there's been no hint of degradation (nor, alas, binder rot). I tried to toss it in the fire (when my baby wasn't looking) and lo, it's fireproof! I ran it over with my tractor and my baby wiped the tire marks right off with a tear-soaked diaper. I've tried drilling holes in it with the post-hole digger and have broken as many drill bits. Even "accidentally" flinging it out the window at 65 mph didn't dispatch it. So, you can feel good about your investment. Make a little space next to *The Devil Wears Prada* and get this in your summer beach bag!

-Wally

PS: It also makes a nice sand scoop or sandcastle drawbridge!

Got a question for our columnist Wally Nichols or just want to buy his copy of *Where Is Baby's Belly Button?* without putting your credit card info online at Amazon.com? Contact him at cwn4@aol.com.

Extra Hug (December 2012)

Dear Hattie,

Today I hugged you extra hard. Harder than normal, in fact. You pushed my head away, annoyed that I had used up my allotted public display of affection at the front door of your pre-K school. "Dad," you huffed, stamping down your snow boot with exploratory defiance and effervescent independence, "Enough. I already know you love me."

You might have even rocked that eye roll we've been working on!

In your hands, some crystals to show your friend and the bagged lunch I made for you. On your head, a woolen cap with two eyes that makes you look like a rabbit. That's the picture of innocence I want for you.

At some point in your fragile years the news will seep into the cracks of your awareness that just a few days before this day, a classroom of children was tragically upset in a small, seemingly safe town. Among the stomach-turning aspects of this story to all of us parents right now is that it could have been any town in America. Including ours. Those of us with access to TV and the internet are hearing the details of these sweet little kids. What they looked like. Their names. What they dreamed of being at the tail end of the journey they were just starting in school.

You will learn that little children lost their lives in what was supposed to be just about the least dangerous place. Chances are good their parents gave them a smooch and hug that morning, just as I have, with just as much love, and then sent them in. And then went to their jobs or home.

You will also learn that in the face of very bad people, very good people sacrificed their lives to mitigate the horror while it was happening. Other very good people have spent lives, careers, trying to keep you, and me, and everyone be safe and healthy in the first place.

But it's a big job.

Whenever we get to facing it, this is an event that will take an extremely long time to fully process, yet we all will have to do it at some point because it is part of the human condition, much as we wish it wasn't. And it's complicated.

My instinct is to cover your ears and eyes and fiercely preserve your innocence. To let you be scared just of monsters under your bed, not monsters in your school.

I want you to skip over to the dramatic play area, or sit crisscross applesauce in your learning circle, or paint with friends, or see how high you can swing on the swing set before Miss Jen scolds you, or pick over the broccoli I made for you at snack time.

I want you to know that almost everyone you meet in your life will at least be good, some really, really good, and that they will care to treat you the way you should be treated and the way I hope you treat others. I want you to know that school is a safe place.

My heart aches for the parents in Connecticut who do not get to squeeze their little children ever again and that, Hattie, is just one of the reasons you are suffering the apparent indignity of my overt love for you this day and every day hereafter.

As if you were not already the most insanely precious person in the world, what happened in Newtown, Connecticut is a stark reminder.

And that is gonna cost you an extra hug...

-Me

Unicorn. Got to have one and got to have one fast. Dodged a bullet at Christmas. (Santa's sleigh was overstuffed with presents for kids around the world, so no room in it for a unicorn, not even strapped to the sleigh's roof rack. Not even a baby one—not that I want to be the dick who yanks a bleating baby unicorn from its mama, but I probably would if I could corner one and if it meant keeping my well-behaved, polite and certainly deserving kid even happier.) My ability to skirt the topic is temporary, and moreover, unicorns are right back in the spotlight as soon as the plastic Christmas toys snap and the uncapped markers run dry.

My daughter requests that when it comes, it comes in pink. (This predilection of hers can pretty much be superimposed on everything these days.) She mentions that ideally, it would be a Pegasus unicorn.

And she gets a blank stare from me.

She has to explain that a Pegasus unicorn is a unicorn that can fly. Hmmmmm. An upgrade (apparently) from your garden variety unicorn which is hard to procure on a good day, even for the dastardly resourceful. Not impossible because nothing is impossible. I'll scream it from the top of any mountain—I BELIEVE IN UNICORNS!! There, I said it. And it only took me 47 years. And screw it, I BELIEVE IN PEGASUSES (PEGASI?) TOO!

I've gotten into the habit of retorting to her age-appropriate requests to have this or that ridiculously expensive or indulgent thing with an equally middle age-*in*appropriate snarky slather: "You want Malibu Hot Tub Barbie and Pool Boy Ken? Well I want a unicorn! And a Caribbean island…"

So there…

Pegasus. I can sort of put the pieces together on that etymology because I buy gas at Exxon Mobil and a Pegasus/flying horse is their well-known mascot, sprinkling mythical dehydrated horse/pixie dung on top of an otherwise sludgy cocktail of MTBE, toluene and ethyl benzene. The gas I buy here feels enchanted.

I just didn't know a Pegasus could be accessorized with a horn. Or that a unicorn could come with wings. Then again, what do I know? "Oh," I said after a furtive Google glimpse, "A Pegasus? You mean the winged-horse god sired by Poseidon, the God of the Sea? Pegasus whose brother is Chrysaor, whose mother was decapitated by Perseus, and who, while trying to get back to Olympus was transformed into a celestial body and sling shot in the sky by Zeus?" Some of this I fractionally remember from school, but the numerator is lean and the denominator chunky. "Dad… *What* are you talking about? I mean a Pegasus. A flying horse. (Insert playful eye roll.) With a magic horn and with magic wings so it can fly really high.

"Ummm, right."

"Have I been a good girl this year? Is Santa watching?"

"Indeed you have, sweetheart. Christmas has just ended, but Santa's always watching."

"You said he goes to the Caribbean after Christmas."

"I think I said *I* wanted to go to the Caribbean after Christmas. But maybe he's there too, unwinding."

"Will I get a unicorn?"

And I start wondering out loud if Santa might get better fuel economy with less of a sled drag co-efficient if he swapped out the eight reindeer for Pegasus unicorns, a suggestion that horrifies my daughter. I add that the sleigh team unicorns' horns would have to be seriously filed down for the benefit of the guys immediately in front when they encounter air turbulence and that at least gets a laugh.

"Wait, you want a unicorn or a Pegasus? Now I'm confused. You did just say unicorn, right?"

"A Pegasus unicorn. And one that is alive. Not a stuffed one. So I can ride it."

She is neither bratty nor demanding. She is stating her wishes firmly as she scratches out a rendering of the mythical beast on a scrap of printer paper that she has snatched from my office printer for this express purpose. She is assertive and knows what she wants, which is a snorting, saddled up, magic-hoofed, real live Pegasus unicorn that is pawing the ground and ready to roll. This is actually what I want for her. Minus the actual living, ground pawing, snorting, unicorn part. But the conviction and tenacity parts? And the wide-eyed immersion in fantasy and mythology? I like those parts.

"But you already get to ride a horse sometimes," I offer. It's an anemic offering, considering...

"I know, but he doesn't fly."

"But what if you accidentally pop a hot air balloon with a unicorn tusk when you are up there riding it," I say pointing to the clouds.

"Dad, I'm not going to pop a hot air balloon. I'm a good driver. And also it's a horn."

"Huh?"

"You said 'tusk.'"

"Oh. Right."

She has a point about the driving. She sits on my lap in the driveway and steers the car while I tickle her armpits. We haven't hit anything yet and she's been at it for a couple years.

Now I have dinner to make so the conversation lulls as we drift to the kitchen.

So this whole unicorn or Pegasus or mutation thereof presents a logistics/fulfillment issue that not even the mighty internet seems to be able to solve. It is, I explain to her over dinner later, extremely difficult to procure a unicorn. Her enthusiasm goes unabated.

"You mean a Pegasus unicorn."

"Yup. Even harder."

"What about Tractor Supply?"

"Won't find unicorns there, honey," I say gingerly. And then as I chew my food and heft an eyebrow, I concede, "But they do have a lot of stuff there." Then I figure out the unicorn part. Or at least the very best I can do with limited resources.

Take one calm family dog, one empty toilet paper roll (spin it off to "empty" if you need to), one chinstrap made out of duct tape and to this, add one rich imagination. Bada bing! Everyone's happy (except the "unicorn" and maybe the next person stranded on the can with no TP).

As for the Pegasus/flying part? Gonna need all of the above, faerie wings, some pixie dust, a patient dog, and a trampoline. There will be air...

-Wally

SERIOUS PROBLEMS

Coffee Addict

Dear Wally,

I think I may be a coffee addict. I literally feel plastered to the bedroom wall in the morning until I have had a few cups. And lately it's taking more (and stronger) coffee to achieve the same results. Without coffee, there is zero morning productivity, predictable constipation and all around grouchiness. I am afraid to quit and afraid to not quit. I've become the ass, as it were, chaffing under Juan Valdez's poncho-covered, coffee-bean filled saddle bag. Here's how bad it's gotten: Starbucks closes at 10pm. When I drove home late last night I had serious thoughts about hurling a brick through the plate glass window and looting. And I don't mean the cash register.

-Got a Problem

Dear Got,

Yes you do. First piece of advice: Don't go busting up a Starbucks. The coffee in prison is weak and cold and you'll have to join a gang to get any.

It is ironic (no?) that I myself am reviewing your cry for help within the walls of an internationally known coffee empire. Let us call it the Mothership. Let us say it hovers over all humanity, and let us further say it casts its menacing green and white shadow on us hapless pawns. Finally, let us say that the place is friggin' packed.

Let me take you on a trip, not unlike Dickens's Ghost of Christmas Future did to old man Scrooge. Come with me to this place and consider that there is an empty chair in this madhouse (besmeared with coffee stains) waiting for you if you don't change your ways.

There's an elevated amplitude of energy in this frenetic place. I'd say a "dynamic" but that suggests presence across a spectrum of highs and lows. There's only one speed here, and ma'am, it is hyper. Clanging plates, loudly dropped spoons, nervous giggles, fingers impatiently running through forelocks of hair. Pacing, snorting, huffing. Banal comments about the weather. Wedding rings being twisted at 60 rpm. Agitation. It's like an asylum.

I'm the only one drinking decaf, apparently.

To my left, a young, itchy man mostly sits. He speaks in choppy, electric sentences and scans the room like a newly released convict. He clutches a Venti Whacka-Chino and slides it around like he's a goalie in an exciting air hockey game at little Joey's Bar Mitzvah. His right leg bounces up and down under the table incessantly as if he were pumping the imaginary accelerator of a neglected farm truck to get it to start. It is impossible to not notice (and to not eavesdrop) as his flailing arm and full body twitches are borderline spastic. His voice is pitchy and his whine piercing. These are the bite marks of addiction.

If aliens landed and took him as a specimen, I'd be embarrassed for mankind.

He makes a scrappy, high-octane plea to his luckless, well-presented female date, insisting *The Empire Strikes Back* is the best film EVER. (No, seriously.) Based on recoiling body language, and a few of her subtle verbal clues (like "I'm sorry, what's your name again?" and "Ummm, what time do you have?") this prowling coffeehouse advice columnist/sleuth can reasonably deduce that it is a first date. And thanks to the unleashed horsepower of his mega-sized coffee, the unfortunate way the conversation has been unilaterally hijacked to Hell, this sleuth can also safely wager this will be a last date. And coffee is to blame. Lots of it.

You hear me??

Wait. For Godsake he now looks like he's playing "Whack-a-Mole" at the carnival with his uncontrollably bucking, steel-tipped workboot.

Cut it out, dude. You are making ME nervous.

Over there, at the fixins' bar, a cross-eyed (bag?) lady leans the full weight of her upper body on the blond maple countertop. She mutters to herself and coos to the heavy cream container like it's a furtive lover as she pulls a lever and coaxes cream into her mug. Then she sighs a deep, postcoital sigh. Rightfully so, people are cutting a wide swath around. This, too, is the picture of the coffee addict one latte beyond the Rubicon.

In the corner, a large man is holding his belly and groaning. Diagnosis? Coffee guts. This happens when you've baldly ignored your limits. The sloshing inside feels like oily bilge in the bowels of a trawler which is getting swatted around on the North Atlantic in November. I can see the damage in his eyes.

Is this who you want to be?

So learn from the Ghost of Coffee Addiction Future and change your course. (Insert rattling chain sound HERE.)

Toward that end, I have scratched out a self-help empowerment script which I implore you to use in moments of weakness on your journey to liberation.

You: "Coffee, go. I do not need you. You are dead to me. (Insert Howard Dean-esque primal presidential scream HERE). Your rich, sensual, roasted aromas repulse me. Your once-comforting womb-like warmth is now frigid and unwelcoming. The sweet ritual of being with you for a few precious, calm moments at the start of my day is now tedious and under it I labor."

Take four deep breaths and then continue with:

35

"Where I once regarded you with the sunken, red-rimmed eyes of a junkie, I now look at you through bright (insert your eye color HERE) eyes with contempt and disgust."

"I don't need YOU to feel alive." (Keep telling yourself this particular line.)

"Coffee, GO. I will pick up with your anemic bastard cousin, Decaf, and we'll make the best of it, even if it means gimping."

Good luck.

-Wally

Got a question for our advice columnist or just want invite him out for a cup of coffee to reiterate that he has no future as a motivational speaker? Email him at cwn4@aol.com.

Overthinker

Dear Wally,

I find myself worrying a lot these days. In part it is just a tendency to think too much about stuff that hasn't happened. Any advice?

-Overthinker

Dear Overthinker,

No need to worry, friend. Here's why: At any given moment, you are either at peace or you are agitated. If you are at peace, you have nothing to worry about. If you are agitated, you are either agitated by something that has happened or by something you think will happen. If it happened already, you have nothing to worry about—it's already done and you've already experienced the worst and that exact scenario will never happen again. If you think it is something that will happen, it will either be something you do, or something that is done to you. If it's something you think you'll do, you have nothing to worry about—change your thoughts or change your actions. If it's something you think will be done to you, it'll either be good or bad. If it's good, you have nothing to worry about. If it's bad, it'll hurt or it won't. If it doesn't hurt, you have nothing to worry about. If it does hurt, it'll either be emotional or physical. If it is emotional, you have nothing to worry about—change your thoughts to reflect (to love?) the reality of that moment because that is what IS. If it is physical pain, it'll either be quick or drawn out. If it is quick, you have nothing to worry about—it'll be over before you know it. If it is drawn out, it will either suck or be ok. If it's ok, you have nothing to worry about. If it really sucks it will either kill you or make you stronger. If it makes you stronger, you have nothing to worry about—that's what we all want—strength in as many forms as possible. If it kills you, however, you'll either pass into nothingness or into an afterlife. If it's nothingness, you have nothingness to worry about, which is to say, you have nothing to worry about. If, however, it is an afterlife, it'll either be reincarnation or Heaven/Hell. If it's reincarnation, you don't get to choose so you have nothing to worry about (unless you come back as a cherry-red urinal cake in the men's room at a rest stop on the New Jersey Turnpike, in which case see footnote below). If it's not reincarnation, it'll be Heaven or Hell. If it's Heaven, or some version of it by a different name, you have nothing to worry about. That's the end goal for many, and even if you don't believe in Heaven per se, and you are wrong, there will either be something for you to do or not. If there's something for you to do in Heaven, you don't have to worry—it'll be heavenly. If there's nothing for you to do in Heaven, you still don't have to worry—you are in Heaven (sit on a flippin' bench and do nothing!). Alternately, if Hell's where you are off to, so be it. It'll either be cold or hot. If it's cold (cold as Hell) you have nothing to worry about— you've already survived a few Ulster County winters and specifically these last few weeks. If it's hot (hot as Hell) you also have nothing to worry about—you've already survived a few Ulster County summers.

So, see? By taking a breath and stepping through the logic flow chart, you can see you have nothing to worry about (except my logic).

Now speaking of thinking too much about stuff that hasn't happened, which is the source of much grinding worry for all of us, I'm reminded of the story of the guy whose car broke down on the side of the road late at night. With only a farm house for miles and miles around, he starts walking in that direction and convinces himself that the farmer is going to be scared and not open the door, or that the farmer will tell him to move down the road, or call the cops on him as a trespasser, or not give him any food or shelter or help, or not let him use the phone. The guy gets himself so worked up and pissed off at what he's convinced will be the farmer's reactions that when he finally makes it to the porch and rings the front door, he's huffing mad and as red as a beet. When the farmer opens the door, the guy with the broken-down car just winds up and punches him in the nose.

Good thing I'm a professional advice columnist. Here's your take-away: Don't punch a farmer!

-Wally

Footnote: If you come back as a cherry-red turnpike urinal cake, you CAN start worrying—I got nothing that'll help other than the hopeful thought that you'll be "re-reincarnated" in less than a week (that's been my observation at public restrooms anyway). With any luck you'll return next time as a higher life form.

Got a question for our advice columnist (who is also a farmer), or have something for him to overthink for you? Email him at cwn4@aol.com.

Selling a Saab

Dear Wally,

I'm having trouble selling my 1989 white Saab. Three unsuccessful listings on eBay. I even lowered the reserve to four dollars and no one's biting!?! How might I word an ad to make it move?

-Saab Lover

Dear (last living) Saab Lover,

Look, someone listed his diseased large toenail on eBay, and after a three-day bidding war (!?!) some other someone walked away with it for $130. Why your very reasonable reserve of four dollars hasn't been met for this one-time luxury motor vehicle is beyond me. (That's over 32 toenails if you are counting at home.) Try the personal, full-confession ad, maybe something like this:

1989 Saab for sale! We named her Tess. Her Regan-era lines remain bold and classic. She'll look great under a tarp on YOUR lawn while you figure out how to get rid of her.

We think Tess is a "she," but honestly have never looked under the hood—not even to check the oil! We also think she might be a Republican.

She starts right up if you first hit her rear bumper hard with a piece of firewood. The key broke off in the ignition (which was poorly designed to be between the seats on the floor and thus get packed with food crumbs by Americans). As a result you now have to use needle nose pliers to get her going. Not a big deal—just set down the morning coffee and have at it! Make sure you are wearing insulated gloves and remove wedding rings and other conductive jewelry so they don't accidentally arc and melt your fingers together. Also if you have a pacemaker, you might want to let a friend start it for you. Park on a hill for trouble-free, pop-clutch starts.

Plan on short trips until your nose gets used to the very bad stench—it's like a forgotten quart of heavy whipping cream or some squirrel rotting or burning or both. Come to think of it, this punky effluvium gets right up in your face with the unbridled, manic, pushiness of a just-rescued castaway.

One huge feature: She's a convertible! So you CAN outrun the stench—and that's where the turbo really helps! One drawback: the roof (recently replaced) is frozen in the open position. As a result, I'd rate the tan interior as crappy. (I do mean "crappy," as a flock of Canada geese seem to have used it as a high-altitude drop zone on their way south.) Quite a bit of inclement weather has toughened up the old girl, including the four feet of snow that fell into it this winter and then melted (I had no intention of shoveling the *inside* of my car as well as the walkway, thank you!).

The barn cat has been sharpening its claws on the recently replaced canvas roof (damn cat) and as a result, Tess now has some classic "laugh lines." (In the interest of full disclosure, the leather seats have been julienned by this berserk feline and her razor sharp claws. The damn cat has also taken up residence in aforementioned roof fabric, but I think a spirited shakedown cruise with the top down (like you have a choice) will dislodge most of the embedded hairs.

There's a small leak. Not sure if it is serious because not long ago, the puddle underneath disappeared. Maybe it is self-healing? I hear Saabs are good like this.

There's a sizeable dent in the passenger side door because we took it out into a cow field and were T-boned by an irate bull. (How's that for irony? We had just been out for steak dinner.)

She used to be a great car. We'd go out for a drive and have the wind rush through our hair as we sped to the ice cream parlor on a typical summer night. Now we just want it gone (just like

GM). We're done. And I'm bald. Plus the ice cream store closed.

Buy this car as a parts car for your other working Saab or drive it up on cinder blocks, shove a flag in it and call it art. Or simply gather some marshmallow-wielding friends, and torch it!

Oh, the friggin' cat gnawed on the steering wheel. Couple pulls of duct tape and she'll be fine.

Good luck and I hope that you or someone wins this auction.

Please, if you are bidding from Monrovia, or some such, don't waste my time. Shipping is over $10k. And on a four-dollar car, well, you do the math. Take your scam elsewhere!

Also—not looking to trade for an unused wedding dress and engagement ring (we've been asked). Not willing to barter for Slavic tutoring. And definitely not interested in lowering the reserve to three dollars.

Free delivery available if you live downhill and there are no turns.

Oh, almost forgot—this car comes with a cat thrown in. (Literally.)

Will sweeten the deal with a toenail if I have to.

Good luck and happy bidding!

-Wally

Got a question for our advice columnist or just need him to sell something for you on eBay? Contact him at cwn4@aol.com.

Leaky Oil

Dear Wally,

I really need your advice on what could be a crucial decision. I've suspected for some time now that my wife has been cheating on me.

The usual signs... phone rings but if I answer, the caller hangs up. My wife has been going out with the girls a lot recently, although when I ask their names, she always says "Just some friends from work, you don't know them."

I stay awake to look out for her friends' car, but she always walks up the drive.

Last night she went out again and I decided to really check on her. I parked my Harley Davidson motorcycle next to the barn and then hid behind it so I could get a good view of the road when she came home.

I was crouching behind my Harley and noticed that the valve covers on my engine seemed to be leaking a little oil. Is this something I can fix myself, or should I take it back to the dealer?

-Steve

Dear Steve,

Leaking valve covers (easy to fix yourself with some chewing gum and sawdust, as the fellow who sold me his car did 200 miles before I took ownership) can spell worn piston rings, unseated valves, an exhausted gasket and/or waxing compression loss. These, en masse, often portend the end of the line for the "engine" (as in the metaphorical "engine," that I'm gonna guess is your soon-to-be-former marriage). That's the bad news. The good news is that it sounds like you will soon have plenty of time to tinker on the motorcycle, and maybe even teach yourself a new language (French, perhaps?) which you can use to seriously ratchet up your new online dating profile. Now remember, a Harley that spits up or leaks nasty old oil is not the right tool for attracting the next mate (is this even what you want??) unless you fancy a HazMat Spill Response Officer in a jump suit who may or may not be the coddling, understanding, lovey-dovey type. So, fix that hog and fly on down the road in every possible sense of the phrase.

Bon courage!

-Wally

Procrastination

Dear Wally,

I have an exam coming up and I'm sick of studying. I'm at a point of diminishing returns. It's costing me 95 percent of my energy to get the last 5 percent of info into my head and I find myself procrastinating. I'm out of things to straighten up and underwear drawers to arrange as I diligently avoid my studies. I figured you (of all people) would have some tips on how to run out the clock on real work. And I mean that in a loving way—my husband and I are big fans of your column.

 -Jane

Dear Jane,

Well, I love you too (I guess). Are you kidding? This entire *Dear Wally* column is one big study in procrastination! I'd say become a columnist for the local paper but the gig is taken and I need the money. (Plus the hate mail reminds me I still have a nervous system which I also test by grabbing onto the electric horse fencing every now and again. YEP, it's working!!) You need fresh ideas. You (and your back-handed compliment) are right. I, of all people, have some tips. Here ya go. No charge.

Typically when I'm faced with a looming deadline, the first thing I will do is… Go online and check my email! Even if you just pick through the tripe and individually relegate the spam-flavored, penis enlargement solicitations to the trash with grumbles, sighs, and sanctimonious indignation, this is a failsafe way to stave off real work and, if handled properly, can gobble up hours, thus pleasantly eroding any hope of productivity. Related, if any of the emails contains a hotlink to the internet, you are screwed. Well, "screwed" that is, if you have any intention of not going down the rabbit hole of the internet head first with your legs sticking out and flailing.

There have been times when I wanted so badly not to do something that I decided to see how much water I could chug in fifteen minutes, and then how many times (and how much) I would have to pee in the next two hours. This, by the way, is graduate level, Advanced Procrastination. And slightly disturbed. Try some of the other things below first.

Whether or not you have children, eliminating the names you definitely would NEVER name your unborn, (never to be born?) kid is time well spent when staring down the barrel of an unprepared for exam. Aldo? Nope. Bartholomew? Nope. Jebediah? Nope. Wally? Nope. You get the idea. Also works on runner-up names you might consider if you decide in retrospect that you screwed your kid's name up and it's time to fix that situation. (Hint: Their school won't like this. There will be raised eyebrows…)

You can always while away a few hours imagining you are dictator of a banana republic. Would you have the death penalty? And who would get it for what? Tailgating? Ahhhh, yes, maybe… Would you make people drive on the left side of the road, or wear top hats, as a tip of the hat to the bygone predilections of imperialist colonialism? Would you allow Cuban cigars? Would citizens be forced to wear different-colored socks? Dictator fantasies are almost as distracting time sucks as lottery fantasies. Engage in them prudently.

There's only so much that one can fit in one's navel. Start a list. Two lists, actually. One for solids, one for liquids. Then start a list of things that DON'T fit in your navel.

In the face of my own looming deadline, and in search of some way to avoid that particular reality, I recently recounted all the things my dog has eaten that have caused him to hurl. This list, which is not short, includes a tube sock, a Lego piece, a spent diaper, part of a picture book, and scraps from the table (this never boosts my cooking confidence). Even his own food!?! Now this is a head scratcher—to see my dog wolf down his dinner, (the same kibble he gets every day for breakfast and dinner) and then start the full spine arches, the low "huhh ahh" "huhh… ahh" of a retching GI tract in distress and ready to return topside, the partially adulterated contents of its stomach—stuff that looks pretty much the same coming out as it did going in.

Make a list of names for male genitalia! Aldo? Nope. Bartholomew? Nope. Jebediah? Nope. Wally? Nope. You get the idea.

Think about, if forced, how many hotdogs could you eat in a half hour…

Recount the names of prior sexual partners and how far things went. (This is good for getting through extreme turbulence in an airplane when you think you are gonna die. Write this list on the barf bag if you are not already using it and make sure your spouse doesn't see it, or you may well die anyway.)

It's always worthwhile spending some time trying to remember the quadratic formula. ($-B$ +/- (sq rt BxB-4AC)/ 2A???) Crap. Who knows? Who cares?

Inventory the freezer. Clean the ice trays. Check inspection dates on stored batteries. Consider which is bigger: Norway, Sweden, or Finland.

Ask a friend to sit down with a piece of paper and a pen. Give them five minutes (or as many as they want) to list all fifty US states. It sounds easy but it can't be done.

And the most obvious, which you have already done: Write a *Dear Wally* question, then sit back (doing nothing) and wait for the response. I'll eventually get around to it.

Now get out there and get nothing done!

-Wally

Got a question for our advice columnist that doesn't require a math formula or an immediate answer? Email him at cwn4@aol.com.

Syrup Worthy

Dear Wally,

I am trying to figure out how much and to whom I should give some of the precious maple syrup I made this winter. I have about three gallons ready to go. It does make a very special gift, but I'm not sure this liquid gold is good enough for just anyone. What makes someone maple syrup worthy in your book?

-Laurel

Dear Laurel,

I understand your dilemma and subsequent proclivity to hoard. For those unfamiliar with the New England sugaring down process, it is quite labor intensive. The maple sap gathering window is limited to just a few weeks in the early spring when the nights are below freezing and the days above freezing. It is in the crook of that thermal differential that the sap runs freely. In this short window you must drill maple trees in excess of 16" diameter, shove in nylon drip collectors which you have mail ordered from Canada in advance, set five-gallon food-grade plastic pails on the ground to collect the run, check daily, bring the contents to a cook-down station which you must also fuel, and then hurry up and wait as 50 gallons of sap boils down to 1 gallon of syrup. Not a process for the impatient. But that effort is what spikes its inherent value. You can be sure the Rubenesque Mrs. Butterworth is not sitting there cooking down her caramel-colored, high fructose corn syrup. Not even close.

I have a similarly sized reserve in my own icebox and it makes me feel rich! It's a strange currency to be trading in. That is until you see it on the shelves for two dollars per ounce.

When you show up as a guest at a party, the go-to gift is a bottle of wine, perhaps a fistful of herbs or tomatoes if you are a gardener and the season is right. Rare (and extremely welcome) is the guest who presents a glass container of maple syrup.

I spend a lot of time studying a would-be recipient. I look into their souls and see if they are syrup worthy. Elaine from Seinfeld did this to potential lovers with her limited stash (14 jumbo cases, for comedic effect) of contraceptive sponges. She had a lifetime supply, even for a porn star, and yet was still stingy. With syrup in considerably shorter supply, we need to be even more discriminating and judicious than Elaine was.

Such a tight inventory of syrup has to be reserved for the truly special, helpful, beloved or needy. It's not to find its way into the unappreciative mitts of one who might be profligate with it. Or one who is just as happy waltzing Mrs. Butterworth around the pancake dance floor. For starters, if you are a churchgoer, you'll want to pour 10 percent of your stash into the collection plate. Tithing, I think they call it.

Then, for the other recipients...

Have they pulled your half-charred body from a burning building? Have they saved you thousands of dollars in taxes? Neutered your cat for free? Have they gotten your undeserving child into a college far beyond the child's ability? Did they get you a new transmission at half price? Pull a tick from the unreachable zone between your shoulder blades? Fix a flat in the pouring rain? Give you CPR or the Heimlich maneuver? (Assuming you actually needed either.) Gently set you on firm emotional terrain? Fix your sciatica when no others could? Plunge a stubborn toilet while others skulked away?

Here's a formula: Take what syrup you have amassed and split that amount in half. Find eight-ounce glass bell jars and fill as many as you can with half your processed syrup. Then spend six months giving half away in line with the parameters set forth above for syrup worthiness. That should take you to mid-October with three-quarters of your original batch (half plus half of the other half), less the amount you personally consume. Then from mid-October to New Year's Day, give out the balance that has been earmarked for gifts.

Whatever is left you can bundle up and send out to any ol' advice columnist you want. In so doing, you will make space in the fridge for the new batch you are about to collect and cook down.

A cautionary note: I love grapefruit. Love it so much in fact that I'm hesitant to eat it because then it's gone. (Note to self: will have to discuss that with the therapist.) Now, I've never said I make sense, so bear that in mind. Recently, I found myself throwing out the very prized grapefruit I had been exalting and fawning over for a full week. I was awaiting the perfect moment, which is the on-ramp to hoarding. Once pink and full of promise, I loved it too hard and too long and for my restraint, it turned into inedible mush. No quicker way to feel like a chump then to throw out what was a perfectly delicious grapefruit because you were too scared to eat it. (Actually, buying a truck full of rocks always makes me feel like a bigger chump.)

Get out that waffle iron and start using it up!

-Wally

PS: I recently learned that maple syrup drizzled on grapefruits is a delicacy. Who knew?

Got a question for our advice columnist or just can't find enough (or any?) syrup-worthy friends? Email him at cwn4@aol.com and he'll back the truck up.

The End of the World (GULP)

Reader,

I have to be careful even writing this, as I am in a public place. If someone were to lean over and filch a peek, they might think I'm scratching out some manifesto of doom and have me removed, reported, deported, detained, screwed down, snuffed out, arrested or water boarded. Me, I'm just sippin' decaf and peacefully considering the imminence of December 21, 2012 (also the winter Solstice) that the Mayans (long since gone themselves. Did they predict THAT too??) had pegged as the last day of their calendar, and which we, or at least some of "we," have come to interpret as the last day of *our* calendar. As in *finito*...

If this comes to pass, and the world ceases to exist on December 21st, I will be pissed. For starters, Central Hudson is supposed to pick up my aging freezer the day after as part of their appliance upgrade program. This is the second time I've set this up because they neglected to call two hours before arriving the first time and I wasn't home. I will get $50 for this exchange and I'll be damned (possibly literally) if I'm denied this windfall by some inconvenient Apocalypse. I am NOT rescheduling this again which is probably a true enough statement whichever way this whole End-of-Days thing breaks.

There's also my dentist appointment just before Christmas. Regardless of whether or not we as a race survive this doomsday, or the next one, you know our teeth will (they survive airplane crashes!?!). So I want them at their very best. Chomp chomp chomp. (Unless the way we end is to be submerged in Coca Cola, in which case our teeth will also just dissolve.)

I have other things I need to get in order before mankind's extinction. I was thinking that seeing my child off to Kindergarten in September, and then later, watching her graduate from college would be super deluxe. That gives her and me about 10 days at this point to cram in a lot of standardized testing, touch on a few of the important points in life and hit a few frat parties. But with enough coffee, I think it can be done.

To be fair about it, there's been End-of-the-World cage rattling before. In fact, for a world that has supposedly been doomed to smithereens so many times before, we're walking amazingly upright. One loopy personal Jesus on the side of Routes 44/55 frantically waved me down as I road-biked on a Saturday evening a few years ago. With wide, wild eyes, he screamed at me that mankind (the whole of it) wouldn't live to see the next day, and that I'd better repent, NOW. (Me: "You seriously stopped me for this? Jesus!... *Jesus?*")

Just before I swung my leg back over the rail and put my iPod back on, annoyed for the wasteful use of my brake pads, I asked him, "Dude, you think I can slide in under the wire at this point? Really? Sunday is only five hours away (and I haven't a thing to wear!!). It seems disingenuous on all fronts and at a minimum disrespectful to HE WHO SMOTES. You don't think that any religion I grasp at now will whiff the reeking false piety of an eleventh-hour charlatan desperado in bike shorts? Am I not better off being in the 95th percentile in Hell than in the 31st percentile in Heaven?" (Ah HA! I did learn something from my high school guidance counselor!)

And off I went, yee-hawing my way to the front of the line for the Hell Express, as far as he was concerned. My final words to him, delivered over my shoulder and whilst shifting gears upwardly, were, "I'll see ya in the underworld, Bro. I'll be standing by the life-sized Justin Bieber cardboard cut-out, eating uncooked fish, reading the *New York Post*, and getting mayonnaise funneled down my gullet in between me talking at people who can't hear me and/or won't listen." Which is pretty much my Hell, if you are curious. Oh, that and being around people whose sockless feet smell like Frito's Corn Chips. (You hear me Cousin Bubba?)

That lanky, lithesome, bell-ringing soothsayer is still out there on the side of the road flailing and pacing and warning, though nobody (myself included) has the constitutional fortitude, or the time frankly, to engage him and debate the hard chronology of his failed prophecies. What's the point, really?

Here's how he is right, though: By screaming "You are going to die tomorrow" every single day, one day he (or his anointed heir) will be right.

Or if you are Mayan and you want to just cast a long shadow of fear, because the end of the world is pretty much the scariest thing you can leverage besides Lindsey Lohan driving your child, AND you have a really long roll of papyrus that stretches out from the 5th century BC to December 21, 2012, you go to the end of the paper roll and put a big X. Then you sit back and wag your finger and say to your people, and your oppressors, "Beeeeeee-have!" (And say it just like Austin Powers does.)

In the case of the Mayan prophecy of doom, they don't really offer anyone a last-minute salvation upgrade package, so we're all fairly screwed no matter how tight we squeeze our particular religion or teddy bears.

I can promise you this: If the world ends on December 21st and there is a Hell, and we (or at least some of "we") find ourselves there, I will make sure the first few copies of the new and improved *Blue Fire and BrimStone Press* are free!

Come find me in the corner where they stash the flippant. I'll be the one in shorts.

-Wally

Fear of Flying

Dear Wally,

I'm afraid of flying. While it isn't a crippling phobia, I've become increasingly uneasy about it. I've tried deep breathing and laying off the caffeine preflight, but these don't seem to do the trick. My kids have their Gameboys and my husband has his book, and they could care less about smashing into a mountain at 600 mph. I sit there and think about the wings coming off, or the plane just nose-diving to the earth. For me, never does the time go as slowly as it does on a plane. And every time I step off the plane, I feel like I've cheated death.

Any advice?

-Fear of Flying

Dear Fear,

By that logic, every time you breathe, sit in a relaxing bath, or even laugh, you've cheated death. A fear of flying is more common than you might think, and by saying that I hope I offer palliation with the idea that you are not alone. In general, we feel better when we think there are others around us who have it as bad as we do, or worse. Which sounds meaner than it actually is. It's about safety in numbers and being appreciative of what you have in light of what others don't.

52

There are some whose fear of flying is so intense that they will only drive or take the train or stay the hell home. Travel has inherent limitations in that case. You are not one of those folks, it seems, and you can take solace in knowing your free will hasn't been so severely compromised that you can't taste the sweet fruit of cultural exploration which awaits you on the other side of the plane ride. Still, that offers little help when you are strapped into seat 19F and sweating like a whore in church (not my expression).

There might even be enough aerophobics on any given flight to have an impromptu emergency support group in the back of the plane. You'd have to identify each other in some way more predictable than looking for all those folks chowing on their fingernails, guzzling whiskey, scratching out a last minute will on their barf bags, or frantically taking inventory of the assorted body parts they will have to claw their way over to get to the emergency exit first, when need be. Cell phone developers make note: Localized airplane panic attack support group app? Send and receive a local distress homing signal text? Too techy? Too creepy?

Let me speak to your flying fear from a quasi-engineering point of view. It's just not the case that airplane wings come off. It may feel like it when you hit that turbulence over the Rockies, but if you look at the staggering amount of real-life proof, there's no amount of acrobatics from bumpy air that would shear the wings off. You may crash into a fireball, but take some comfort in knowing that the wings will still be on! (Umm, am I helping here?) And unless you are flying one of those decommissioned 727s we sold to the Congo in the 1960s with no spare parts and no service manuals, you're not gonna just drop out of the sky (though you might want to avoid a discount airline around the Himalayas). So check that stuff off the worry list!

Planes are designed to fly on one engine, so if one craps out in flight, you'll still have one to get down really quickly (and I don't mean at 32 feet per second, squared, which is how fast a coconut falls out of a tree, absent friction).

My Engineering professor used to laugh and tell us, "Doctors kill 'em one at a time. We engineers kill 'em a plane load at a time." Don't listen to that kinda stuff.

I went through a phase where I overanalyzed the physics and aerodynamics of flight. Silly me. I did so without adequate information and with a runaway imagination of the various ways Bernoulli's principle of fluid dynamics might suddenly fail, or how some Jihad terrorist might be squatting in a cornfield somewhere in the middle of America with the underbelly of my plane in the crosshairs of his shoulder-held rocket-launcher thing. As if there are terrorists in Iowa... That's what you get for switching majors from Engineering to English/Creative Writing.

Perhaps you dread losing control and just freaking out in that claustrophobic plane? You won't, but even if you did, you'd be wrestled to the ground, have a tube sock stuffed into your mouth, and be restrained with a belt by irate fellow passengers. You'd then be stuffed in the cargo hold so quick your kids wouldn't have time to look up from their Gameboys. And they'd have to pick you up, mummified with packing tape, at the baggage claim.

But I assure you, it's good not to go there intellectually. Instead, stay in your seat and think of the fine time you'll have at your destination when you arrive in just a few hours. Close your eyes and imagine having sex. (Even better, imagine having sex with that lunk next to you, your husband!)

I think you'll be ok. If you are not with me, my sister swears by kava-kava, a calming Indonesian pepper tea which will stink up the plane but not as badly as a full barf bag.

*

Good luck, and wear a helmet (advice I give everyone in every situation).

-Wally

Got a question for our advice columnist, or just can't bear to get on a plane to the Caribbean, but don't want to waste the ticket? Let him have it! Cwn4@aol.com.

PS: Did I just lose my job as an advice columnist?

WORLD CLASS ADVICE

Olympic Gold

Dear Wally,

I'm all fired up about the Olympics and want to know if there is any sport I might have a crack at next time around. I'm a mid-40s male with a herniated back and a slight beer gut.

-Jack (High Falls)

Dear Jack,

You sound like a shoe-in. I can't believe I'm not already watching you on TV! Seriously, when you say "next time around" do you mean next Olympic cycle or your next life? I too wonder from the safety of my couch, every four years like clockwork, what sport, if any, I might be able to participate in on this fantastic international stage and do my country proud. Winter or summer makes no difference to me, though all things considered, I'd prefer to make my contribution in shorts, and not the tight ones the divers wear either. As I watch grueling displays of inhuman strength and balance such as the gymnast's rings, I keep a pen and paper handy and put a solid "X" through my (and it sounds like your) dwindling list of viable options. A 40-something fellow with no serious athletic experience could still be ripe fruit for, and thus catch the eye of, a forward-thinking, savvy coach on the prowl for new talent. But the Olympics are traditionally a young person's sport. However, there is something to be said for our extensive life experience and gravitas.... You'd probably have to increase your exposure however, and get out there with your skills, whatever they may be, whenever you figure them out. I suggest starting out rollerblading naked with an inflatable camel along that paved pedestrian stretch of Route 209 to draw some attention…

A couple of thoughts that might help eliminate some dead-end alleys... Vaulting: You need a 15 mph vaulting accident like you need a hole in the head (which is what you'll probably get with even one misstep). Leave this act of hurtling into a stationary object to the gents with eggplant biceps and the ultra-nimble, petite tumblers. (I've had orders of onion rings that weigh more than some of those Russian gymnasts.) I'm guessing you and I have no business on the floor routine mat unless we're being rolled lengthwise to mop up someone else's sweat. Running: Well there really is nowhere to hide from the camera (and global humiliation) if you are having a bad day. A bad day is not being able to run as fast as your car goes. Even 20 feet behind the pack makes you look like you screwed up and are running the wrong direction in a different race. Diving: If you can get past the dental floss Speedo bathing suit, this might be an option. You have gravity on your side so you can't screw up and go the wrong way off the platform. Be aware, though, it will take at least three more Olympic cycles to unlearn the cannon ball, or at least to successfully petition the Olympic committee to reconsider the 10 meter free-fall Shrieking Water Displacement Bomb as a serious sport, as they have done with Beach Volleyball. (For real?!? With the curious amount of prime time network coverage volleyball has received, I keep thinking I've accidentally stumbled onto reruns of Bay Watch. It might be in play for you, so long as you get a few injections of steroids in that lower back and leave the spikes to your partner, Bambi.) Shot put: Easy to practice at home for this one. It's called cleaning out the garage. Put the dumpster 30 feet away and let fly.

As for winter sports, well, your financial barrier to entry will increase by a few dollars—you'll have to get a warm parka and goggles (as I frequently warn *Dear Wally* readers to wear anyway). You'll want to avoid downhill ski racing as they reach speeds of up to 90 mph and often seem to have neither control nor contact with the earth. This type of activity is not covered in your health insurance, I'm pretty sure. Hockey is too much of a team sport and so you'd have to share your gold medal with others. I know at this age, that's just not what you want. To my mind that leaves only one sport. The perfect sport. Bobsled. Here's my proposal: You and I go to the Salvation Army and pick up a sofa (aka sled). We hump it up to the US training grounds at White Face Mountain and see if it fits on the iced track. If it does, we're so in. I'm betting there may be no two more experienced sofa jockeys out there. With gravity doing most of the work, and your bad back, the remaining fine tuning necessary during the harrowing last two minutes of our lives will come from our vast reserves of experience driving this inanimate object. We could be onto something with this and return gold to the coffers of our national pride's treasury (plus whatever coins are between the cushions). Whaddya think? I'll start looking for some parkas, you start stretching (out). Next stop, Vancouver! It's all downhill from there.

Yours in gold,

-Wally

Got a question for our advice columnist? Or need a partner for your Olympic-bound team? Contact him at cwn4@aol.com or visit his blog, www.wallynichols.com.

Starbucks Order

Dear Wally,

Yesterday at Starbucks I ordered a nonfat, triple-venti, half-caff, caramel-laced, mocha-frappuccino, dolce macchiato with one shot of Costa Rican organic shade Terrazu, fair-trade, light-roast Americano decaf drip-drizzled in the center. I then asked for a double shot of Guatemalan Casi Cielo dark roast espresso and Ethopian Sidamo poured clockwise and circumferentially around the inside edge of the same cup (my own creation that I've cleverly named "the ring of fire"). I mentioned to the excessively pierced Morning Barista Associate (MBA?) that if possible, my beverage should have dual pumps of sugar-free Juju-boo nut syrup, squeezed between the inner thighs of virgin Cuban farmers and, if there's a benevolent God, He might further bless adding one pump of vanilla syrup (not one shot which is typically three pumps, but one single, sublime, subtle and superlative pump). While He's at it, He might as well leave behind a cane sugar swizzle for my benefit. And, finally, I intimated that this dreamy concoction be presented in a doubled-up, bleach-free, "green" white recycled paper cup "system" to go because the insulated cardboard sleeves that typically sheath the single cup delivery units typically don't stay on for me, and because waxy brown corrugated cardboard is best used for packing fish in ice on the docks (not insulating or sleeving my drink, thank you).

Well, the Barista froze up and looked at me with glazed orbs like she was some doe I had just jacked with the high beams of my gold trimmed H-3 Hummer. No further words or movement came from this wispy, wan thing. The solid brass door knocker she had obviously stolen from the front door of some Transylvanian castle (and then pierced her nostrils with) didn't even budge. Did my simple drink request break her in two?

-Cal

Dear Cal,

You sound like a right fine pain in the rump. I don't think I (or anyone) can help you.

-Wally

Afraid to Skydive

Dear Wally,

I want to go skydiving but I'm petrified. I'm in the throes of a reactive midlife crisis (relationship-based) and skydiving seems clichéd. I also have control issues and a slight fear of heights.

What do you think?

-Alan

Dear Alan,

Slight fear of heights? Oh boy.

Whatever happened to the good old-fashioned midlife crisis that involved buying a red Corvette, getting a hair transplant and banging your 25-year-old secretary? I guess the answer is parachute technology has improved. But I still miss the golden days of socially deviant behavior!

Well, you have come to the right place for pointed pontification on skydiving as I have recently done it, under similar circumstances, and have a bird's eye perspective. Actually, while falling at a rate of 1,000 feet per five seconds, from 13,500 feet, I think I actually kicked a bird in the eye, which lends some authenticity to an otherwise tired expression. The kick was inadvertent, of course—I was busy testing Galileo's principles of acceleration (32 feet per second/second) in a nauseating barrel-roll/sissy-girl scream and couldn't afford the time to be kind to animals. I'll do something nice to an animal later. Like order a veggie burger.

I'd been meaning to hurl my body from a perfectly functioning airplane for many years and the universe, with all her fickle variables, lined up in one recent, crystal clear morning. So fuck it, I went.

The staff at Skydive the Ranch in Gardiner, New York was shockingly calm in the presence of this jittery first timer. I expected sober reverence, but instead found jocularity. "Hey Buster! Yeah, YOU packing the chute, chop chop. Pay more attention!?!" I felt like shouting, but they were on it, as if they do it every day. Which they do. By virtue of the fact that I am writing this, we have empirical proof they did it right.

They led me to something resembling a moonshine-distilling shack which instead has high-tech parachuting gear in it. For once, being in a jump suit actually suggested I was going to jump, versus paint a boat or something. Three colors (fantasies?) to choose from by the way: Airplane-mechanic blue, prison-inmate orange and DWI roadside garbage picker upper neon yellow. I'm only a little nervous that they have so many of the unused mechanic suits available. Oh well.

I walk like an astronaut in my Borat bathing suit nylon harness to the waiting plane, which is an old thing from the '60s (so am I for that matter) that has been gutted and retrofitted with two astro-turfed benches and a very wobbly, 6'x6' plastic garage-style door toward the back, out of which all 20 of us in the plane will soon plummet. No inflight peanuts on this trip. No barf bags either.

It takes 15 minutes for the old girl to claw her way to 13,500 feet and I notice that what was a sunny day below has given way to snow flurries up here. It's the end of April!?! Damn this never-ending winter of '11. At 90 knots, I'm told, snow will feel like getting shot in the face with rock salt. Cool!

My harness is strapped at four points to jumpmaster John, a 30-year-old adventure guide with a pleasant demeanor, nice teeth and a mountain-man beard. He sits directly behind me. He's so close I can feel the whiskers. Suddenly the plastic garage door is exactly where I want to go. By myself. He swears he has a girlfriend, but I'm feeling that right now, I am her.

I'll have this guy, a complete stranger, right on my back for over two miles of skydiving and the pictures of us say it all: I feel like a hen getting drilled into the dirt by a horny rooster. But this relationship, normally burdened by terrestrial gravity and social convention, will soon and temporarily feel detached and light. And free. It will also save my life. This is a mandatory surrender of control, but, ya know, for the best.

You'll want to get your head around that concept, all you control freaks thinking of tandem skydiving...

Standing on the edge of any abyss is a daunting scenario. It presents questions of an existential nature, like, "Wait, what the hell am I doing?" and "Did I do my will right?" It's funny, for all the time I've been in commercial planes and wondered if a parachute would save my keester in a Hollywood pinch, now that I have one, at no time do I ever feel nervous in this plane. Not only can I jump out, I will have to.

Below me are 100 stereoscopic, panoramic miles of earth-view. The Gunks look puny, if you can imagine that. I have climbed them with ropes and, with my cheek mashed against the cold conglomerate, I've felt rightly humbled by their magnitude.

Here, with my toes on the last two inches of supportive tin engineering can offer, I have an existential choice: I can be sucked out of the plane or I can jump. I mean this in a figurative sense as the mechanics of detachment are more passive. You arch and on the count of three, let go. After the first second, the plane is already hundreds of feet away. Talk about crossing the Rubicon... But spiritually, this is the quintessential instant of definition for a midlife crisis. You, Alan, can be active or passive.

For me, it was important to not be a victim of these circumstances that I had chosen. It's an interesting balance of control (nothing pressured me and nobody made me do this after all) and surrender (I can't do it myself if I expect to survive). That applies to the circumstances we find laid out and squirming at our feet, too.

The lessons to be learned here are as profound as the serenity of falling away from the trinkets of mankind's ingenuity and toward the noiseless beauty of Earth.

The details are too fine to perceive from this height, and that's for the best. This is the free fall so few will choose to experience. The big let go. A full minute later, at 6,000 feet, you pull the ripcord. You, Alan. Not someone else. And thus begins the struggle of gravity against your resisting body. It's so quiet you can whisper to your own God and still be heard. The details pull into focus. Like Google Earth on Fast Zoom, but with a wedgie and no mouse.

The Gunks start to look majestic again. You see rooftops, make out shingles, blades of grass and then, before you know it, you are back on the ground. Feet in the easy dirt. You have landed and nothing is broken.

And as an added bonus, you release the harness and get the monkey off your back (no offense, John!)

I say go for it. I can't be the first person to tell you to take a flying leap! The worst that happens is you live.

-Wally

Want to watch Wally take his own flying leap? See it here: http://www.youtube.com/watch?v=ClmIGm8FAyI

Summer Camp

Dear Wally,

My 13-year-old nephew, Gardner, is going off to summer camp (Camp Flying Cloud) for the first time. It's a "wilderness camp" in Vermont and he's never really spent much time outside. He's more of a Gameboy-and-ice cream kind of kid. (No matches allowed, the mail comes in once a day in a garbage can, and they have to forage for food and nonpoisonous berries, miles from the nearest road, etc.) Any advice on how I might write a letter to console him? I'm really fond of the kid. I don't want him to get jungle rot, or dysentery, or malaria or get mauled by a wild animal. Help!

-Uncle Charlie

Dear Uncle Charlie,

This camp business sounds like the classic bait and switch—they sell the underage kid on a "wilderness retreat," then make him and his friends hunt and trap on their Vermont woods so THEY can survive the winter. And then charge the parents for the experience! They avoid providing food or shelter or WiFi by spinning it as "green." Wow. What a scam! It's called an underage labor camp and the International Labor Organization has strict regulations on such things. But seriously, rest easy. This will be an experience he will remember for the rest of his life. He will draw on this well of resourcefulness for many years and bond with the other inmates, creating lasting friendships (Bloods? Crips?). You are the only one worried here. Let it go. Fire off a volley of support that touches on the things 13-year-old boys care about, to wit: Bathroom humor, fear, and your own experiences at summer camp on the way to manhood.

Anyhoo, here's a letter template for you! Change it as you see fit:

Dear Gardner,

Welcome to summer camp. I was going to send you a jack knife so you could kill something wild but your mom said no knives were allowed. Are you supposed to use your fingernails to scratch out the eyes of a charging grizzly bear? Ummm, good luck with that. (I suggest screaming like a girl and shoving the kid next to you in its path.) If you get mauled, don't blame me, blame your mom who wouldn't let me help you defend yourself.

She also said you don't have any matches to start the fires you need to cook.

What the...?

How much is this camp, anyway? Do you get a hot pot and a generator or are you rubbing two sticks together like a hobo under the interstate bridge? Fire by stick, as a business model, didn't work for the Neanderthals—they went extinct and their women were extremely hairy. Lesson learned (finally). I've enclosed a lighter. Don't let the guard see it.

You are welcome.

Do you get water, or do you have to make that too? If so, remember the formula: two parts hydrogen, one part oxygen. Don't screw this up or you will burn off your eyebrows.

What about a solar powered soft-serve ice cream machine? Should I try to mail you one of those or won't it fit in the daily mail garbage can?

Do they put mints on the rock you use for a pillow when room service turns down your bed of moose urine soaked twigs at night?

Your little sister Whitney says she misses you.

NOT.

I bet the feeling is mutual. She has taken your room and is living in it. I heard she painted it pink and put your Gameboy on eBay. Don't tell the other campers you will return to a pink bedroom with a Jonas Brothers poster on the wall or you may well be hung up by your underwear on a branch in the pine forest and left to rot (at least that's what happened to me).

Look out for wolverines. They are rare in Vermont but if one escaped from a Russian zoo, it would probably head straight for Camp Flying Cloud... If a wolverine gets you, can I have your bike? I hear wolverines seek out small boys sleeping in tents and eat them from the inside out. Sweet dreams.

When I was a kid I went to Camp Itchybutt. It was fun. (Until I got kicked out for mooning the girl's camp.) (And stealing the motorboat.) (And sneaking into the kitchen and eating the Captain Crunch.) (And lighting my farts.) (And lighting my counselor's farts when they slept.)

I'm sure your experience will be much richer. Plus you probably won't get dragged down to the lake and beaten with the oars by the older campers. That part of my camp experience wasn't in the brochure...

This will be a unique, life-forming experience. At the end of your three weeks you will probably realize that a desk job after college maybe isn't all that bad, versus being out in the wild, eating poisonous berries and getting crippling diarrhea.

Well, I hope you make it out alive. I'm rather fond of you.

Hey—if you scout a good place out there in the wilderness to slam up a Walmart, let me know so I can buy the property and clear cut it!

Like I always say, "What good is nature if there isn't a nearby parking lot to view it from?"

Love,

Uncle Charlie

-Wally

Got a question for our advice columnist or just want a pep talk for your camp-bound kid? Contact him at cwn4@aol.com.

Winning the Lottery

Dear Wally,

What should I do if I win the lottery?

-Dreamin' Dan

Dear Dan,

When, baby, when! Drive your mid-80s Toyota Tercel with the fender that flaps in the wind out to the Grand Canyon. F that. Hire someone to drive that car out there. You take the private jet and meet him there. (After you're pampered at the Canyon Ranch Spa, of course...) Back that piece of sh!% up a small incline near the canyon's sharpest, most dramatic edge until the wheels start spinning because you are giving it the cactus enema it so richly deserves. Then, with little emotion, step out, lay a heavy rock on the accelerator, and hear its pansy engine whine for the last time in your 20-year relationship. Step back and consider this caterwauling inanimate object that has so often failed you in your moment of need. It might have the good karma to get melted down and come back as lunchboxes for small indigent school kids, but YOU are in charge of its fate this go-round because YOU have the million bucks. As the engine squeals, a few nature-seeking tourists in ridiculous "expedition" pantaloons shoot you a toxic glance. You don't care, you can buy THEM. The chassis rocks back and forth, grunting with ambition. You know if you were on the Thruway and asked this crapbox to perform at 5,000 rpm you would soon be engulfed in flames on the side of the road and stopping miles of traffic. Now this thing is scrambling for a lifetime of forgiveness. Too little too late. You won't fall for it again. All you need to do is grab that gear shift and drop it into drive. (This fantasy tastes so good you forget to notice that you have mowed over one of your wife's favorite flower beds. No worries, mate, with your mil you'll buy her a new one, and a neutered male gardener, too, in white gloves.) You reach through the driver's side window of the Toyota, past the twitching, redlined tachometer, and you grip the gear shift. This is it. Go time.

BAM! You wrestle with the gearshift for the last time ever. It still puts up a fight, as somewhere 200,000 miles ago you inadvertently left second gear in the parking lot of Emmanuel's supermarket. You step back making sure your toes are out of the way. (Ummm, that would suck.) The front wheels start chewing the dry, caked Arizona soil. They can't get enough. Dust is flying, the engine is howling like an orgasm-ing banshee. Your arms are folded with contempt as you watch this iron turd make its final advance. It scrambles for the canyon's edge unaware that in seconds its pathetic, unreliable life will be over in an arching swan dive you and your million bucks have orchestrated. It occurs to you that you have never seen this thing move with such gusto. Since Day One it has robbed you of ever having the thrill of driving, even momentarily, in the passing lane.

It hits the lip and sails gracefully into space. Its poorly balanced frame quickly heads down, rear end first. This moment is sweeter than you had even imagined. You squeal with delight as you run to the edge and watch. "Take that!" you scream, shaking your fist. The canyon mocks you with her echo, "Take that, that, that, thaaaaa." Silence, as nature engulfs man and his folly. A bird chirps. "Piece of sh!%" is the final epithet you mumble through the sun-scorched lips your recently hired man-servant forgot to balm. The vehicle disappears out of sight. In your pocket is the incriminating title of ownership and the tin VIN number you pried off the dashboard with a screwdriver so the authorities can't trace this leper car back to you.

You jump back from the edge expecting flames to lick up the entire two thousand feet from the bottom and singe your eyebrows (her fuel tank holds only six gallons. Check that, you giggle, *held* only…). Your new BMW is waiting. The seats are air conditioned and your driver has a cold beverage ready for a job well done. The canyon's mighty maw has consumed your troubles without the slightest reflux. Being rich is wonderful! You have trouble remembering what life was like back in the bleacher seats with the riff-raff.

Then, the hiccup. You are pulled over by park rangers as you try to exit. You command your driver to take evasive measures and beat Johnny Law. He tries, but is quickly surrounded because these government drones are underworked and over-resourced (and overflowing with Federal Law Enforcement goodies that your lottery tax dollars helped pay for. Grrrrrrrr.).

You are presented with a hefty summons for littering (turns out the engine block has a second VIN number stamped into it for this exact purpose—damn it all!!), a two million dollar EPA fine for polluting the Colorado River with gasoline (a two thousand foot freefall and it still didn't explode?? What the heck...?), and, finally, a fine of $590 for killing a tour donkey (a class A misdemeanor in Arizona which also carries up to thirty days in jail. Thirty days is a long time to not take a shower, you think. Worst case scenario...).

Good luck and remember what your uncle says: The lottery is a one dollar tax on the stupid. (He won't get a bloody cent when you win! Not if. When.)

-Wally

Want to share your lottery winnings (or lottery fantasy) with our advice columnist? Email Wally at cwn4@aol.com.

Shoveling Snow

Dear Wally,

I'm a little older and find shoveling snow to be a real pain. Any ideas on how to get someone to shovel my walk for free?

-Sandy in Accord

Dear Sandy,

Here's what I did: I took out ads on Craigslist and eBay. The copy went something like this:

"Snowbank available to good, loving home at deep discount. Bidding starts at $13. You must move it. Please bring a shovel and some energy. It is in perfect shape but I no longer need it and feel I can't properly care for it. It is located right by the house, so from where you park your truck or minivan, you'll need to clear a path 75 feet long and 2 feet wide, pretty much right to the house (and as long as you are here, would you mind casting a little salt or sand on the path you will be creating, for your own safety?). You will be amazed by how loving and peaceful this snowbank is. And smart! And obedient. (We asked it to stay a few days ago and it hasn't budged!) It has other beneficial "green" features like saving refrigerator energy by cooling your beer and lunch meats for free. Hurry, this offer expires in two days (or the first few days the temperature rises above 32 degrees). The first $13 takes it! Serious inquiries only."

In so doing, Sandy, you'll ratchet up perceived value and make folks feel like they are getting a deal in these times of fiscal austerity. Plus you'll get gone a snowbank for which you have no more need. And there will be at least $13 extra dollars in your pocket. Lastly, you'll get a shoveled walk out of the whole happy transaction.

I've also auctioned off used moustache parts on Craigslist for fun (!?!). The questions that come in are rich:

"Do these parts come with a manual?" (No.)

"Are crumbs included?" (Yes.)

"Are the moustache parts still growing?" (What exactly do you mean?)

"Have the parts been regularly washed, conditioned, and deloused?" (Yes, yes, and no.)

"Can I use them on parts of my body other than my upper lip?" (Excuse me? Like where?)

"Is it a unisex moustache?" (?????)

"Does it work in the winter?" (Yes, down to minus twenty Fahrenheit.)

"What size batteries does it take?" (Ummm, double A, I guess. But it's mostly solar.)

"Will you consider a trade for a mid-80s Camaro and an engagement ring?" (I'm guessing this is why you have an available engagement ring...?)

"Will you ship overseas?" (Don't they have hair over there??)

I've also auctioned a 60' diameter pond, 8' deep ("Free to good home, water not included, you must move. No reserve!") just to see what would happen. Fifteen calls.

You would be surprised at the power of the internet and the doors it opens to the global market place for products and services, if you can polish the turd so it is juuuuuuuust shiny enough...

I knew that any job could be filled, there existed a buyer for anything, and as Disney Corporate says (and as a result, my Disney-infiltrated nephew repeats robotically), "Dreams really do come true" when I saw a few years ago a piece on CNN featuring one fellow who advertised on eBay (and promptly sold at a bidding war) a diseased, no longer viable, large toenail that had finally given up the ghost and come off at the gym. He tucked this fungused thing into his sports bag, took some pictures, and whammo!, it was up on eBay. Ewwwwe. It's probably on some freak's mantle in Guam right now. But some happy freak. My bigger point is that you should be able to make someone very content with your snowbank if you present it correctly. And you'll get that walk shoveled! That's what you wanted, right?

"But Wally," you may say. "I don't have a snowbank to offer in the first place to get my walk plowed! What do I do about that?" And to that I say, "Sandy, you ARE IN LUCK! I happen to have a snowbank you can have. It's right by the house and it's really nice! Come get it. Oh, and bring your shovel!"

-Wally

Free WiFi

Dear Wally,

I am one of the many mobile office workers that can be seen in those coffee shops around the world that have the good sense to offer free WiFi. And as a member of this growing class of café customer I would like your help in liberating us from our second-class status among those cafés that place restrictions on customers of my kind, setting aside designated (non-ideal) tables and/or time limits on our stay. As I've achieved "regular" status at many such places, I suspect that the mobile-office worker outperforms the leisure class dollar by dollar, that we provide a reliable midweek financial support and the comforting sense of a filled dining area. But most importantly, it needs to be said that a person can just as easily "hog" a premium table reading *The New York Times* or having endless loud debates with fellow retirees. In fairness, I should mention my fellow laptop jockeys who are, I suspect, in violation of etiquette when they add the Bluetooth to their mobile office, broadcasting their business conversations in a way that makes the café feel too much like one of my old temp jobs, as well as those who neglect to tip in recognition of their almost free workspace. So Wally, as I hope to see a long-lasting and mutually beneficial relationship between the café owners and the mobile worker, I ask you to put your wisdom to this 21st century ethical grey area.

-Ken Vallario

Dear Ken,

You kidding? Starbucks and Panera have become the de facto washrooms, mobile offices and pieds- a-terre for the homeless. The more unwashed the better, and just wheel that friggin' overloaded shopping cart right in! (Don't want anyone to steal it!) No hassle from coffee shop management either, far as I can tell, which is as it should be. All members of the public should be treated equally. Speaking of pieds, I saw some guy washing his feet in a Starbuck's bathroom, and I kid you not, sir.

So why is management breathing down YOUR neck after a mere 30 minutes of WiFi use or relegating you to the crap table when they see you pop your laptop? It's because you are too clean. Or you smell too good. Or they think you won't have a freak-out in public. I can help you with that.

Murky territory, this whole internet *thing* as my grandma used to say, even 12 years into its explosive existence.

Culturally, we are still groping through the protocol, etiquette, and social convention of what is publically acceptable as it relates to technology and communication. Even language (that old lumberin' lady) has taken a broadside hit from the battering ram of fast-paced technology. I'm not sure kids any longer know how to actually spell out "Oh My God." Maybe a few. Maybe not.

Eating establishments, including coffee shops, have long clung to the basic premise that nothing succeeds like success. An empty restaurant is a diseased restaurant. A commercial pariah. Might as well hang a twitching rat over the front door.

They need patrons. And you, Ken, are a patron.

In this respect, there is power in your very presence at the coffee shop! You might well leverage that. Furthermore, from a basic economic point of view, it's a winning bet that sooner or later, you (the freeloading guzzler of the same gimmick that was willingly offered up to bait you in the first place) will splurge for a coffee. Then a muffin. Then a breakfast sandwich.

This piecemeal revenue stream, multiplied by however many days it takes for you to finish your damn novel, will ultimately serve them well, as I suspect you know and as I suspect they know too, deep down in the batter.

I doubt there's enough of a correlation between tipping the serving staff (which should happen regardless) and management's curdled attitude about excessive WiFi usage to adversely affect the joint's WiFi policy. Email, et cetera, doesn't unduly throttle the typical coffee shop internet server. (Wait, by "work" by any chance do you mean downloading enormous piles of steaming porn? That would bog down the coffee shop server, to say nothing of being frowned upon. Doubt that's your situation—just a heads up to other would-be, socially deviant, WiFi pigs!)

So treating you as a second class citizen is fairly myopic and it's crazy that some establishments still don't see that clearly. They will, but your hiney may well be stealing WiFi and sipping coffee elsewhere.

Their efforts would be better placed snuffing out annoying one-way phone calls. It is astounding to me that people still think it is ok to have a loud phone call in public. As I write from my table tucked into the corner (which may be second class but I chose it), I am hearing one deafening conversation between a couple, and a second, emotionally charged, phone call to a client. All far too loud and far too inappropriate.

Excuse me one second, Ken.

"Hey. You on the phone INSIDE THIS CAFE… shut your BACON HOLE!!"

Seriously. Who does this still? (Except that I just did).

Patience, grasshopper. Oh, crap. I have to go. Been online for a while now and the manager's heading this way, arms folded. Ooohfah!

-Wally

PS: You might just ask them how they can be so sure you are actually USING the WiFi. Couldn't you actually just be, ummm, writing?

Got a question for our advice columnist or just feel like he has used up his 30 minutes of free air? Email him at cwn4@aol.com.

Hotel Soap

Dear Wally,

When is it ok to steal soap and shampoo from a hotel?

-Jane (Hurley)

Dear Jane,

You mean versus stealing it from a store??

And by "soap" I presume you also mean the hotel's bathrobes, water glasses, TV remote, TV, mini bar (the fridge AND contents), towels, towel racks, bedding, telephone, lamps, curtains, room service menu, furniture, wall art, and anything else that's not bolted down?? (Some folks are incorrigible takers and some folks are incorrigible justifiers.)

So, when is it ok to "steal" from a hotel? Well it's a slippery soap (ba da BING).

I'd like to remind you that you are not writing in to an ethics columnist (or this response would be a lot shorter), but merely a regular guy peddling advice for street survival. A guy who in fact is writing this advice on a barf bag stolen from a recent flight to Florida and with a pen "borrowed" from Heather at the bank when she was counting 20s. (For once the pen wasn't chained to the counter!) And finally, a guy who was recruited out of college to play on the very successful MIT card-counting team in Las Vegas (but who declined because wigs and fake moustaches make him itch and also he loves his knee caps). So bear those bona fides/advice credentials in mind.

That said, load up on the hotel swag. Victimless crime. Go ahead. As a rule of thumb, it's ok in my book to take any vial of shampoo or conditioner or soap or even a Q-tip (high end joint, ehh?) that strikes your damn fancy when staying in a hotel, so long as it is something carried on the housekeeping supply cart and also found in the bathroom. (So ix-nay the room service pewter coffee pot and half eaten Danish left outside the door of someone else's room, tempting as it may be. That's stealing and a little gross, too. Also, no poaching the unattended housekeeping cart in the hall—that's outta bounds.) Finally, if it requires more than two fingers to filch, let it stay (you might consider this advice when nose picking, too).

I know the line of reasoning: You paid for that hotel room and thus that down comforter belongs to you, darn it.*

You can rest assured that 1) the consumer goods manufacturers have either sold the soaps, etc. to the hotel chain with the full understanding (and hope) that they will serve as promotional items that keep "selling" the brand long after the hotel stay, or 2) the manufacturers have outright given them to the hotel (for the same purpose).

In fact, by you furtively shoving them into the dark recesses of your carry-on luggage, beyond the firewall of dirty underwear that no house detective dare breach, and by you being a cosmetics drug mule as you happily whistle *Zip-a-Dee-Doo-Dah* past the hotel's check-out desk, you are effectively saving the marketing department having to pay some college kid in a chicken suit to hand the promotional sample-size swag out on street corners.

It's a win-win in the sense that the hotel provides an amenity (beauty care products, tonics, nards, and salves) and the manufacturers get low-cost exposure with a final distribution cost to your home of zero.

Of course, there's that line which is neither to be crossed nor especially fine. Here's another rule of thumb given to me years ago by a lawyer friend, and the pith of the statement is probably applicable in all aspects of life: If you have to ask if it's ok, you already know the answer. Or this: If your back hurts from taking so much, then you've probably taken too much.

If you are still confused, maybe the best way I can help you is to go along with you on your next holiday and discuss the items on a case-by-case basis? If you are going someplace warm, and it's a fancy hotel with a heated pool AND room service, chances are I'm free!

Good luck, and remember, if you need the soap that bad, you sorta need the soap that bad! I think we're all ok with that.

-Wally

If you have a question that needs answering, send an email to cwn4@aol.com.

*So will the bedbugs that come along for the ride and infest your home! There's no free lunch, especially when it has six legs.

FRIENDS AND NEIGHBORS

Red-Neck Neighbors

Dear Wally,

On the weekends my red-neck neighbors get liquored up and drive through my property on four-wheelers, which sends my dogs into fits of hysteria. I have asked them to stay off my property, but they continue cruising around, often with a beer in their hand and a child on their lap. I have considered calling the police but am slightly afraid of retribution, as I know they are avid hunters. What should I do?

-Riled in Rosendale

Dear Riled,

Most wilderness survival guides suggest avoiding direct confrontation with drunken four-wheelers, especially when they are with their young. Like grizzly bears, drunken four-wheelers are highly protective of their cubs and can become quite irritable and aggressive, especially before, during, or after a long, lean winter. This behavior gets more exasperated when you fold alcohol and internal combustion engines into the mix. You may find yourself with knobby tire marks on your back if you provoke them from too short a distance. You may also find yourself being pelted with empty Coors Light cans, and possibly risk having your buttocks avulsed by an angry swipe of their fingernails.

A box of roofing nails "accidentally" spilled on your property should fix this problem right quick. There's also a product that shoots liquid skunk stink from a two-inch PVC tube that is similar to the aerosol-fueled potato launcher some real rednecks use. This non-lethal weapon assaults the unwelcome intruders with a fine mist of unrelenting pungency that will surely cause them to reconsider trespassing the next time as they ponder their transgressions from a quiet place of occupational humiliation and ostracism. The stink gun is safe to use because you can sit on your porch, pitch in your rocker like Granny McAdams and wait for them to come to you. The thing shoots the mist a few hundred feet, according to the manual. It will feel like fresh morning dew to them. But it won't smell like it!! (Hee hee.)

There is one final weapon available if diplomacy fails and olfactory assaults do not work. You'll find it extremely effective but will want to use it judiciously because once you let it out of the cage, so to speak, it is not easy to put back in. Be warned, too, that the cost to society is high. Here it is: Place loud speakers just inside your property line and start blasting back-to-back versions of Ethel Merman's "There's No Business Like Show Business" and "Everything's Coming Up Roses." Turn up the treble as far as it will go. That'll do it. When they are off their four-wheelers and writhing on the ground in pain, begging for mercy, then call the cops and let the legal system do its job...

Good luck and wear goggles.

-Wally

PS: Avid hunters? Might want to tuck that Halloween deer costume and fake ten-point antler hat back in the closet until this is all sorted out...

Open Letter to a Garbage Truck (and Driver)

Dear Garbage Truck (and Driver),

4:30am? Really? Do you, too, suffer from insomnia? I didn't until I moved here. And hired you. And it's not so much a naturally occurring insomnia, as it is a forced, manmade insomnia. (Do you get my drift? I get your redolent drift...) The thing is, if you were to defend your insanely early arrival at the side of my house by saying there is other garbage that needs to be picked up after mine (perhaps cooler, more intricate or better-smelling garbage than my humble, nasty stuff?)… garbage that need be collected before the landfill closes (and by the way, the landfill never closes), I could understand that by dint of bad luck in choosing where I live (won't make that mistake again, trust me), I'm friggin' FIRST on the list of morning pickups and you will run late if you don't start with me when you do. But everyone I have ever spoken with says they too get their garbage picked up at 4:30am. What's with that?

So, unless you stole Santa Claus' rig AND painted it puke green AND welded on an 80-ton hydraulic compactor to its rear end, how can you be everywhere at once (and by "at once" I mean 4:30 am)?? There are now two ways in which you defy the laws of nature. 1) By being everywhere at once. 2) By getting that lumbering, brick shithouse of a wobbly-wheeled truck you drive up to a speed of 80 mph in my driveway.

Surely in all your years of picking up other peoples' refuse you have saved an alarm clock or two?? How about you wipe the banana peels off it and duct tape it to the dashboard of that monstrosity of a truck you drive. Right up there next to the cup of coffee you had to make at home because even the 24-hour McDonald's isn't open this early.

Maybe you are simply unaware of how brutally early 4:30am is?? Mmmmm? Maybe? Is there nowhere you can go read a book or something until the sun comes up, or at least the moon goes down? The longer you wait, ya know, the more the trash decomposes and settles down, the smaller the load, the less you have to work. Just saying…

And anyway, you come hurtling down my otherwise quiet street threatening every creature foolish enough to be out and about. We share the planet, you know…

That revving, soot-belching, diesel engine that sounds like a rhinoceros with horrific, lentil-based gas… Those squeekin' brakes… That eardrum-piercing beep beep beep that never serves to warn anyone or anything (including the cans you

crash into) that you are in fact backing up until it's too late…
All part of the assaulting cacophonous din you orchestrate
thrice weekly.

It's almost as if you are trying to see how very loud you can
be. Is that possible? Or is that notion preposterous? C'mon—is
there a little bit of you that says, "Screw it, if I have to be up,
so does this bastard…?"

Your truck has tusks in the front, designed to make you look
like part angry warthog, part ferrous devil. This is a self-
fulfilling prophecy, you know. Look the part and you will act
the part. The Italians judge a man's character by the shoes he
wears. Somewhere in this is an apt analogy, though I'm having
trouble identifying it. You know why? Cause it's 4:30am.

When you do finally leave with my garbage in your steel belly,
it's not as the delicate poet Carl Sandburg might have it, to wit,
with you moving out like the fog moves in, on little cat feet
and of silent haunches. Definitely not that 'cause you probably
ran the cat over and who knows how many countless raccoons
too, driving as you do, like a bat out of hell, dripping
yellowish, slick, fetid juices onto the asphalt from the iron,
hyena-strong jaws of your truck's ass-maw. (By the way, I've
never actually used these two words together. Thank you. I
guess.)

I'm not saying I'd like your job, no sir. But if I did have to do
it, and I might someday if this writing crap doesn't work out,
just know that I'd not revel in sharing the misery of forced
awakeness with all my customers at hours ungodly. I might
keep the truck to a low idle. I might throttle back the red-lined
exigency of rubbish removal. It's not like we're diffusing
nuclear warheads before they explode, right?

So, in case I was wrong, and you don't have one, I'm throwing
away my alarm clock, which still works. God knows I don't
need it around here. Maybe you do?? Set it for 7am and let's
see if the world ends!

If I sound angry, I'm not. But then again, you can check in with me when I'm awake.

Glad we could have this chat.

I love you.

-Wally

PS: Why is it that when I drive behind all garbage trucks, the wheels wobble so badly they appear to be on the verge of coming off? Is it from running over all those things like raccoons, cats and garbage cans?? Get that looked at, ok? It makes me nervous. And what happens when it comes time to throw the garbage truck out? Do you drive it into a bigger garbage truck?

PPS: Calm down. I take my own garbage to the dump now. This letter is for my non- Hudson Valley based friend who has complained about the early morning and loud garbage pick-up process in his suburban community. Yet another reason to love it up here!

Need a question answered or a courtesy wake-up call at 4:30am? Email our advice columnist at cwn4@aol.com. He'll be up.

BYOVB

Dear Wally,

I got an invitation to a BBQ the other day and the hosts wrote, "BYOVB." I am vegetarian and so is my husband, so I wondered if this hand-written addendum was for us, specifically. I am assuming that they meant, "Bring Your Own Veggie Burger?"

-Confused

Dear Confused,

As an acronymical phrase-starter, "BYO…" has been so baldly co-opted no one knows what the hell anyone means anymore. In simpler days the second "B" in "BYOB" was booze. That said, my thought now is that VB = veggie burger, not vodka booze.

It's not like you are so freakishly out there that the hosts couldn't even begin to accommodate your eccentric dietary needs… (Or are you difficult in some way you are not telling me? Will you eat only local ground cover or tree bark? I don't know, people are weird about some things.)

A pack of frozen veggie burgers (five dollars) might be a good thing for your hosts to just have in the freezer anyway as insurance for some future vegetarian incident. Supermarkets today have entire sections devoted to simulated meat products, most of which are injection-molded to resemble some shape (a rib cage or what have you) that vegetarians probably are skeeved out by in the first place.

Fifteen years ago my uncle invited me to a family BBQ. He was cooking a whole pig in a pit. I held my nose and attended. It actually smelled really good. (In fact, I love the smell of cooking swine—I once told my wife if I ever cheated on her it would be with bacon.) My uncle knew that I was done with real meat, and mocked me relentlessly for my decision, as many of my good friends still do. All cool and I'm used to it.

Nonetheless, he indulged my "passing" fad (still going since the early '90s as a matter of fact), put on a pair of dark sunglasses so he wouldn't be recognized at the checkout register, and bought a packet of the original Boca Burgers. The way he spoke of it, the shame that burdened him was akin to buying a Penthouse magazine and a five-gallon jug of Vaseline at the local drugstore in front of a bunch of horrified nuns.

Of course, things have improved a lot since then (*Penthouse* magazine comes discretely wrapped, for one) and you can buy

Fakin' Bacon that tastes pretty darn close to the real thing (minus the end-of-life, feedlot adrenalin surge which you can now buy as a bottled spice/flavor enhancer if you miss that zing!). It's no longer a shameful thing to buy veggie burgers. Halleluiah! We're out of the (sub-zero) closet!

But back to my uncle's BBQ... Because that burger was V1.0, and prototypically nasty, I could choke down only one, especially as said uncle thought it would be fun to push it in the pig's mouth alongside the apple and cook it that way. I watched this perversion until I got dizzy. Even the pig refused to keep it in its mouth—it fell out three times before my uncle got frustrated, shook off the dirt, and flung it on my plate.

Afterward he Ziplocked the remaining burgers, and with a smirk, stuffed 'em in the freezer—WAY back and out of sight. He then tipped a beer bottle at me menacingly and warned me that it was my duty to finish the rest of "these damn things" the next time I showed up (or he might use them as pucks for pond hockey). The implication was that "my" veggie burgers were going to somehow defile the meat in his freezer. I've had to bear that cross for a long time.

He has moved a few times in the almost two decades since that day and, to his credit, each time he has dutifully packed up and transported the neglected, freezer-burned, outcast patties to a new part of the country (but the same part of his freezer). My point? Who knows, other than having a pack of veggie burgers handy is a decent idea. It's not like they go bad...

But but but... what if "BYOVB" doesn't stand for "bring your own veggie burger?" What if it is code for something else? Like bring your own veal balls? Vermillion basketball? Vera Wang bowling ball bag? Volkswagon Bug? Vienna Boys' Choir? Velveteen bra? Venison broth?

I guess you must seek clarification from the hosts lest you show up with veggie burgers and insult them because they actually wanted Venetian blinds. That's my advice at the end of the day. So I guess I didn't really help you at all.

Hmmmm.

-Wally

Got a question for our advice columnist or just want to see him daringly rescue the apple from the spinning hog's mouth? Send an invite to your next pig roast to cwn4@aol.com.

Houseflies

Dear Wally,

With the recent Indian summer, we still have houseflies and they are really bugging me. How do I get rid of them?

-Frustrated

Dear Frustrated,

First, "Indian summers" are now more politely called "Native American" summers. As for the pesky, common housefly, try writing a strong letter. I've found that if you triangulate a creative position between complimenting them, threatening them, and articulating your frustration with them, they will usually move on. You have nothing to lose but a $.44 stamp.

I've taken the liberty of drafting just such a written instrument, which you may use, royalty free, if you like.

Dear Housefly,

Before I am forced to dismantle you with a swatter, let us discuss the issue of my irritation like gentlemen. You are wily and focused on your game of torment. Your plump, lethargic brethren, on the other hand, like to hang out by the sweet melon juice I accidently leave on the counter.

Even as the dark waffled shadow of the orange plastic swatter looms larger, they remain oblivious, easy targets.

This need not be your fate if you take decisive action now. Let the following fictional script not star you. Get out of my house, where you pay neither rent nor taxes, and do so immediately before I take swift action with the one-dollar swatter I got from ShopRite last night.

I say you are unique. Educated perhaps? You sally forth with the reeking and abundant confidence of a Cambridge letterman and yet possess the irreverence and gall of a pesky suburban thief. You have been relentlessly buzzing around my head as I work in my office. Are you looking for something in my hair? A treasure? A lost relative? A landing zone from which to jettison your larvae?

You hop from my knuckle to the unpaid Sprint bill on my desk. Why? There's no sustenance here. Then it's off to the arm, then the toe, then the neck. Repeat. Annoying, surreptitious, twitchy.

Why can't you just be a fly on the wall, the wish of so many?

I have a second swatter nearby yet you never sit still long enough to let me get a lock on you. I've been flummoxed by your cunning, again and again.

You go to my right ear. Bzzzzzzzz. I flick you off (no I won't swat myself if that's your game, but nice try). I try to write a few more words and you are back. Refreshed. Regrouped. Ready once more to pester. You buzz around so quickly that I can hardly see you. At first it's just a slight irritation on my skin but it soon escalates to jagged fingernails clawing the chalkboard of my nerves.

It seems like a design flaw of nature. You are obsessed with landing on me like I'm some sort of undiscovered planet. Yet for your needs, I am fallow. You have no tools to penetrate my skin and get my blood to feed yours. And even if you acquired some discarded, proboscis-shaped BP mining tool for that job, time is not a luxury you have. I think you live for, like, four days.

Yet even with no reason to land on this dead, hostile planet called me, you try. Repeatedly. At the risk of sounding paranoid, I am left no choice but to conclude your sole *raison d'etre* is nothing more than to annoy me.

If that's the case, so be it. Game on. Let us do what comes to us naturally so I may mush you and end this folly once and for all. I will temporarily suspend my important life goals of happiness, love, compassion, and productivity. I will instead focus on your demise, as you, and nature herself, have so willfully forced me. Take this message, then, back to your kind and heed it.

What? You are back? Already? You MOCK me? Well let's just see about that...

I hold the swatter with my best hand—the one that can deliver a sizzling first serve on the tennis court every now and then. It's hard to concentrate on writing when... Whap! Damn, I missed. You little F-er... Ok, ok... There you are, camouflaged on the thin edge of my black computer screen. Finally you stop moving for a nanosecond. Enjoy your last second on Ear...Whap! Damn.

Whap! Whap! Whap!

Damn. Damn. Damn.

My wife pokes her head in my office. "Is everything OK?"

"Yes," I growl. But it's not.

Bzzzzzzz. You are back. Apparently your work is not done.

Ok, ok, ok, I reassure myself in a lunatic's whisper. Now I've got you... You have moved to my LED backlit screen which betrays your position. You show up like a broken femur on a bright X-ray. A fly, if I may, on a wedding cake.

Checkmate, you little pecker!

Bzzzzzzzzzzz. You taunt me to no end! If I kill one of you, one thousand more of you come tomorrow. Still it seems incredibly worth it.

WHAP!

Hmmmm.... Housefly? Are you there?

And that's it. An epitaph of milky white visceral pulp smeared on my screen. Nothing a squirt of Windex can't fix.

Do you get my point, Housefly? So now, while the going's good, take your business outside and spread the word.

-Wally (or whoever uses this template)

PS: For the record, let it not be said I wouldn't hurt a fly. And, Frustrated, if letter-writing isn't your thing, fret not, there are only a few weeks until nature's frozen fist will hammer down your problem. Alternately, clip out this column, roll it up like a stick of beef jerky, dip it in honey, and hang it by a string over your kitchen sink.

Priority Male

After 39 years of unfaltering dedicated service, through rain, sleet, snow, hail, and god knows what else, Ira Poppel will hang up his name tag and retire from the US Post Office in Kerhonkson, New York. Below is an excerpt from an unofficial exit interview with our advice columnist, Wally Nichols, conducted in late January, 2013.

Wally: Ira, thanks for meeting with me as we celebrate all the years of service you have given the post office and the American people without once "going postal."

Ira: Thanks Wally. I enjoy reading your column.

Wally: Probably because I've never turned the spotlight on you. You can't hide behind that formica counter any longer, sir! So, 39 years is a long time to be working for anyone, let alone a governmental agency. When you started at the post office they were carrying mail around on horseback, right?

Ira: I don't think they had even discovered horses when I started. Or electricity. The wheel hadn't yet been invented. We just hauled slabs of rock with messages chiseled in them.

Wally: Well that must have been a drag. Get it?

Ira: (silence)

Wally: (throat clear) Are you leaving because Lance Armstrong has brought shame upon the house of Team US Post Office?

Ira: Not really.

Wally: Does the post office encourage the use of performance-enhancing drugs amongst its employees so the mail can get delivered faster?

Ira: Oh my. I don't think so.

Wally: Because it doesn't seem like it. Are you leaving because you are just tired of the same old faces coughing on you every day?

Ira: Not really. They've become friends, some of them.

Wally: So are you just sick of the blue uniform?

Ira: Sure Wally. That's it.

Wally: Favorite subject?

Ira: You sound like Barbara Walters when you say it like that.

Wally: How DO you FEEL about that? Just kidding. Favorite subject has to be the weather, right?

Ira: I do get caught up in plenty of weather-related conversations. It's a safe topic. Calms people right down.

Wally: I can see that. Hard to piss anyone off talking about the weather.

Ira: It's nice out, right? Boy it's hot!

Wally: Ahhhh! You ARE good! I'm feeling calmer already. What's the strangest thing you have ever weighed on the postal scale? And parts of your own anatomy don't count.

Ira: (blushing) Is this interview almost over?

Wally: People always want to know what goes on in the back there. What DO you guys do?

Ira: Poker. And sometimes when we're closed, we'll put on puppet shows using the front counter. Harmless stuff. Punch and Judy. Nothing crazy.

Wally: What do you think you will do with all your free time when you retire?

Ira: Collect stamps.

Wally: Bada boom! You're funny! Hey, does anyone ever shoplift from the little post office store there? Packing tape? Little boxes? Pre-stamped envelopes? It's nice stuff...

Ira: Oh yes. You'd be surprised.

Wally: You'd think someone with those filching tendencies would set their sights a bit higher, like Target or Walmart. No offense.

Ira: None taken. But if you need an envelope, you need an envelope, know what I mean? People do what they have to do. I can usually tell who's gonna give me trouble.

Wally: You guys have baseball bats behind the counter if things get rough?

Ira: No, we have Forever Stamps.

Wally: Does "forever" *really* mean forever? (Now I definitely sound like Barbara Walters!!) Or is the government gonna tell us one day that the "forever" stamps actually need a cute little supplemental stamp called the "and ever" stamp that costs us an additional $.50?

Ira: That's a good idea. I'll mention it.

Wally: Now that you are no longer a postal worker, are you worried that people will assault you because you don't have that $10k fine for assaulting a postal employee protecting you?

Ira: Not really.

Wally: You made it out alive. If someone actually worked for, say, 70 years and dropped dead of old age behind that counter, is there a Priority Mail box large enough for a grown adult's body?

Ira: I'm sure we could find something.

Wally: Would it still be a flat rate of $7.95?

Ira: Yes, except if you were shipping the corpse to Alaska or Hawaii.

Wally: Ewwwwwwww.

Ira: Well, if that's all, I should be going.

Wally: But you're retired! You have nothing to do!

Ira: I'll find something. I have to mow the lawn. Are we done here?

Wally: Yes. Oh, one more thing.

Ira: Yes?

Wally: I forgot my mailbox key. Can you… ummmmm? Last time I'll ask you. Swear!

Ira: You are right about *that*. Good day.

Wally: There you go with the weather again! Do you know that the word inspiration has "IRA" right in the middle?

Ira: Hmmm.

Wally: Ok, NOW we're done! Happy ret-IRA-ment!

Field Guide to Below-the-Belt Insults

I was recently addressed in non-flattering terms by a fellow motorist with a boil of enflamed road rage in need of a good lancing (which I almost did inadvertently with my bumper). It got me thinking about the use of anatomically based insults and specifically the nuances of which one to hurl when. This irate driver with spooked out hair and flailing arms could have strapped his churlish, vitriolic warhead onto any number of available human body parts to insult me, but he didn't. He specifically called me a dick. Turns out, most of the insults we use come from the body's equator, which is to say, below the belly button and above the thighs. ("Use your turn signal, you stupid elbow" doesn't really cut the way it should.)

How hard must it be teaching language-immersion students who are non-native speakers when to use which term… I hope the following examples provide some insight on the nuances for context and usage, though it does seem there are virtually unlimited, situation-specific opportunities to warrant gripping the handles of the insult launch pad. And in this respect, through my field research (and occasional crappy driving) over the years, I'm glad I can be of service.

Calling someone a dick can either mean you love them or hate them. (No one ever said English made a lot of sense.) Delivered with an aggressive tone, clenched fists and beady little eyes, those four letters pack a wallop the likes of which can readily escalate out of control. You rarely get to call someone a dick in this agitated state and not have them respond with commensurate bellicosity. If you go there, you might just as well emphasize the hard "k" of "dick" with a glottal thrust (and some spit?) to maximize the caustic impact. You've got nothing to lose at this point except four hours in the Emergency Room.

And yet, those very same four letters can be used as a term of jocularity amongst friends.

Huh? (Language students are forgiven if they want to snap their pencils in half at this point.)

You are sitting around a restaurant booth and a friend says "pass the salt, you dick." (At least my friends do.) That's totally fine. Might even lead to a few laughs.

You call the person who cuts in front of you at the supermarket a dick. (Note: If YOU cut in front of them, it's because THEY must have been being a dick. Let them know this with a raised middle finger and a scowl, which they clearly and fully deserve.) (Actually, I don't advise taking my advice, pretty much ever.)

Closely related, "prick" is reserved for some deeper level of premeditation and contempt. If the two insults were fishhooks, prick would be the one with the barbs. If a dick is bloated with arrogance (ummm, bad imagery...) or if they are vindictive, then you can escalate them to prick. It's a fine line. You may always pre-charge either insult with a couple extra joules as in, "*such* a..."

In calling someone a wiener, you feather the edges of the dig. It's almost a pejorative term of pity. The cool girls in school might refer to a Napoleon Dynamite type whose glasses are too big (give me a break! It was hip back then!) and who can't move with confidence through their midst, a wiener, or weenie. Think goofy, self-effacing and pathetic, but someone who can program computer code or build a radio, or rock a pair of floods* like no one's business.

Let's pull a Vassgo de Gama (extra "s" intended as I smirk over here) and circumnavigate this particular midsection to the back.

Many people are deserving of the insult "ass" if they are stubborn, rude, stupid, childish or simply disagree with you. Of course it is not gender specific, as everyone is in possession of at least one. Some people have more than one. Besides the lips, it's the second most popular body part to invite someone to kiss.

My friend euphemistically refers to people who are asses as "tail pipes," which is an automotive analogy. You'll buy yourself a couple steps to the door before they realize the insult.

These few words do much of the heavy lifting in conversational English language usage, so learning when to use them is worth the ink. Plus it remains my continual personal challenge to see how many swears I can get away with printing before I am reprimanded by my editor.

-Wally

(On this very subject, ask your English friends what it means when you call someone a "Wally.")

*Floods are long pants that are actually not long enough, thus revealing the ankles and leading some hecklers to believe you are the chump waiting (like a wiener) for a flood that just ain't coming.

PS: I've fantasized about an invention that would be installed in one's car. When you screw up, and actually care to apologize, you hit a button on the dashboard and a sign pops up that the other driver can read that says, "Sorry" or "My bad." Makes sense, right? Right now there's no easy way to admit guilt or contrition on the road and in separate cars, so road rage has no choice but to fester. Of course there would have to be a separate button that makes the sign say, "You are such an (equatorial body part)" or "Pucker up and kiss my tailpipe."

IN NATURE

Open Letter to a Deer Tick

Dear Deer Tick,

Really? *THAT'S* where you decided to dig in? Of all the gin joints in all the corners of the world, you pull a Humphrey Bogart and go to my Ass-a-blanca? Are you brazen? Ironic?* Or just stupid? Do you think I don't scratch down there? Thought maybe I wouldn't recognize your subtle brand of itch and that you'd just slip in unnoticed like that imposter couple at the gala White House dinner? Ha! You picked the wrong place on the wrong guy for that. I spend a lot of time just standing around scratching my butt. A lot. Ask anyone.

I hate you, tick. And all your lecherous, bloodsuckin' brethren. What exactly is your role on this planet? You don't even make a cute pet. No one has bothered to make your likeness into a loveable cuddly toy (Hello Kitty Deer Tick?). Get a real job instead of living off us doers. Sycophant.

I guess you figured you'd get your fill of my B-positive mojito, leave your disease in the tip jar, get out and wait for the next guy, who could just as easily be me again.

Well, too bad. You got caught and your punishment will be having your body separated from your head with a pair of tweezers, no anesthesia.

Am I angry? You bet. I was out for a walk in the woods. Doing something (even if it was nothing), unlike you. You've been waiting for God-knows how long to brush up against me and jam me, you spineless arachnid opportunist.

That's why I have no problem tweezing your head off.

I guess this call for your cruel-as-possible demise reflects poorly on me. We are to be judged by how we treat the weak, yes? Too bad. I will be merciless, judgment be damned. I will unleash the full wrath of my Scorpio birth sign upon you (and I don't mean the medium-grade stuff like stubbornness, moodiness, artistic flare and a penchant for the melodramatic music and black eyeliner of "The Cure").

I'll deploy the big stuff. If we had a mini electric chair for ticks, I'd strap you in it myself and pull the lever while reading a comic book and flossing. That's how little regard I have for you.

Well, there's no commercially available electric chair for you (that wouldn't also hurt me) but we have something almost as good—A Porcelain Chair. And I think you know what I mean. Or you will anyway when I push the flusher and you go for the waterslide ride of your life.

Unfortunately, our red-hot woodstove designed to simulate the scorching underworld you so richly deserve is off for the Spring or I'd drop your torso on the griddle top and watch you sizzle as I prepare for the assault of antibiotics my doctor will prescribe for me because of the red bulls-eye rash calling card you left on my rump. It was hard to spot way down there without an understandably unwilling spouse, but I managed using a contortionist's flexibility and a complicated mirror system tied with baling twine to the family dog's back.

Or maybe you had designs on the gallimaufry of my unkempt head hair as you started up my leg but instead got halfway up and pulled over at what you thought was the Grand Canyon and then just stayed to camp out and sight-see? Well I am not your personal state park. And even if I was, I'm closed due to lack of funding.

Yes I'm mad at you. You are a dirty little schmuck bringing into my house (sneaking through the back door I might add) Lyme's—a multifaceted disease that we cannot cure and one that makes our baffled doctors look like they are blindfolded, drunk and flailing at a pinata with a bottle of amoxicillin tied to the end of a sawed-off broom handle.

You bring unwarranted and unnecessary expense. It is because of you and my feeble health insurance coverage that I will spend my rainy day fund on something other than a rainy day. Not on a new guitar, or a gym membership, or a teeth-whitening system, but on drugs to undo what you have done.

How dare you? How dare you bury your little tick head in my flesh and start eating ME? I should be eating YOU! You are shoplifting as far as I'm concerned and you should be punished. I hope that when most of you lands in my septic system, some bigger tick makes you his "girlfriend" like they do in prison. I hope he dresses you in a tutu and smears lipstick on you and makes you pass out cigarettes to the other ticks I've flushed down there over the years. I hope institutional humiliation and bad cafeteria food await your headless torso.

In 20 years when you have regrown a head and you have figured out a way to escape my family's fetid septic system, I hope you go out and tell your young tick friends about the horrors of incarceration and that they best pack up and beat it out of Ulster County.

Until then, I'm flushing and you are circling the drain. See ya in Miami, Sammy.

Waaahhhh-woooooosh!

Rest in pee.

-Wally

*LOVE using "ironic" improperly—makes me feel fresh, dangerous and alive!

Want to write an open letter to an animal, plant or mineral that you are pretty sure either can't read English or doesn't care? Email our advice columnist at cwn4@aol.com and he'll do the heavy lifting for you. Looking for a part-time job with a poor salary and few benefits? I need a seasonal tick checker.

No More Winter

Dear Wally,

No more winter. Do something.

-Had Enough

Dear Had Enough,

Me too.

So, close your eyes and stay with me here: It is April (in my mind). There's no snow on the ground any longer. (Just viscous, boot-sucking mud.) The saturated ground percolates like a nasty, spent, kitchen sponge. The wild raspberry laterals are a soft, anticipatory lavender. They hash onward through the brittle, stalky undergrowth, their fruit a distant, doubtful promise.

I'm walking down the driveway and the little remaining gravel that hasn't been shoved up on the lawn by the damn plow guy (me!) crunches under my Keen sandals—footwear as optimistic as it is seasonally inappropriate. In the privacy of my own home, I might wear them with socks. Maybe not. Haven't decided yet.

To my right are the feeble remains of what was once a mighty collection of firewood—seven cords big, face-stacked, and formerly impressive. Split and stacked ash is a strange, antiquated currency to trade in, but having enough for the winter feels like obscene wealth against the threat of a depleting, extruded winter and the double-hammer blow of four dollars per gallon fuel oil.

In the nearby garage, where it was sheltered from the concussive dumping of this past winter's snow, the M is parked. Say the letter "M" in the context of hay fields, gardens, or barns, and countless agriculturally minded folks will know exactly what you mean. This colossus of still-cold steel is the same classic tractor I grew up using and it has been in my careful stewardship since I was eight. (The puddle of dark motor oil beneath notwithstanding. Old tractors, like old people, sometimes just leak.)

My M has travelled one hundred miles from the farm of my youth to the farm of my adulthood. She had been too good a friend and too willing a worker to leave behind. That's why she now winters in the garage and my own car does not.

The International Harvester company of Rock Island, Illinois made a few classics, all painted red, and the M is probably the best known. She was forged in America's first-rate, Midwestern manufacturing heyday—pre- and then postwar. Her lines are iconic and elegant. There are no safety features whatsoever. In fact, she is actually dangerous—tippy on the hills with her narrow front wheels and unforgiving with her death-wheelie torque that could easily flip us over and pulp me.

Today I will wipe up the leaking hydraulic oil rivulet from her dried out piston seals with the care one might use wiping the drool off of a cute baby's chin. I will charge up her battery for a few hours, dump in fresh gas, and wipe down the seat. I'll draw out the choke almost two-thirds of the way (which is the sweet spot my well-trained finger knows after so many years).

I'll need only lean briefly on the starter. Three cranks of her mighty four-cylinder, high-compression engine, a gasp of vaporized fuel through the throat of her now obsolete updraft carburetor and she'll jump to life. She'll snort out the off-season's phlegm, rattle off winter, and rock gently in the depressed wheel ruts her own dead weight has pressed into the dirt floor over the winter. Starting like that is a guarantee that few winter-weary engines can make. Just ask your chainsaw.

I'll find first gear (all the way to the left and down) and navigate through (but not over) the garage clutter that has crept ever nearer these last few months.

We'll go for a spin down the driveway, she and I. It'll feel more like a parade. A celebration of Spring. We will go down and visit that first lonely daffodil poking out where our driveway meets the town road. Then, we'll turn around and putt-putt back up, inspecting the rolling fields that, now butterscotch and bleak, will jump overnight to electric green and need to be cut because fifteen horses just can't keep up with the growth despite their 24-hour grazing. It will seem impossible to imagine such abundant life can exist after such monochromatic, flash-frozen dormancy.

Overhead, the honking geese (in flight formation) that gave this town its name will try to acoustically overpower the M and let us know they've returned—that Georgia or wherever is no longer cool. Here, Kerhonkson, New York, is where it's at.

In a few more months, as we near the summer solstice and it's light until 9pm, I'll hook up the M to the thirty-year-old rusty hay cutter and knock down neat, organized windrows of juicy alfalfa and timothy that will bake in the relentless sun and then shimmer with dew the next morning. As evening falls again, you will smell the fresh-cut hay carried on a lazy breeze as far away as Route 209 and you'll hear the orchestral tree frogs conducting the summer evening's nightly concert series.

The M will do all the heavy work, hauling with purpose and pride and efficacy the machines that make a farm work; haybines, rakes, tedders, balers, and wagons. She is the grand master in this parade of steel, grease, and dust—her season is summer.

The horses will barely look up from their grazing—they've seen it all before. This is their winter food being sorted and stored for a time when they are again shaggy and bored and standing near a new wood pile, pastern deep in crusty snow, bathed in the bleached light of the new winter moon.

But first, summer.

Soon.

You still with me, Had Enough?

Hang in, we're almost there.

-Wally

Got a comment for our advice columnist or just want to help him pick up hay for next to nothing but a soaked shirt, a maw of dust, and maybe, just maybe, a glass of water? Email him at cwn4@aol.com.

Global Warming

Dear Wally,

Global warming... What's the real deal? You seem scientific, what with those nerdy glasses and all. What's the big hoo-ha about global warming? I mean, really... Should we actually be scared or is this some silly screwball scam concocted to make us conserve energy? Also wondering, do the initials "GW" in G.W. Bush really stand for "Global Warming?"

-Anonymous in Accord

Dear Anonymous,

First of all, it doesn't take a scientist or even someone with "nerdy" glasses to figure out that "Anonymous" is likely not your real name. But though you chose to hide behind a veil of secrecy, I have ideas about this trendy, hot-button issue that require me to get on my soapbox...

So much ado about global warming, people... The scientific community is wadded up about the Earth's unstoppably rising temperature. Al Gore is thumping his chest like a silverback gorilla and looping film clips of icebergs falling off the polar caps. It makes us feel like we might actually get crushed by massive breakaway sheets of ice at any moment. (Incidentally, that ice is thousands of miles away from the Hudson Valley and would never fit under the Kingston–Rhinecliff Bridge, nor could it go over it because it would never be granted an EZ Pass without a major credit card.)

This fear mongering has got to stop. It may be true that the planet is overheating like an '82 Buick on the Long Island Expressway during Labor Day weekend, but we do have options... despite what the drum-beating, 'fraidy-cats are saying.

America, rest easy. The solution is at our fingertips, and has been for 75 years: If all of us from sea to shining sea just open our freezer doors for a few hours a day, we can cool this scorching orb right down. (Just put your head in for a minute and feel the cold blast!) Leave that freezer door open and the cool air will escape to do its job. End of crisis.

So easy.

There, now don't you feel better?

-Wally

PS: If you want to do more than your part, drive your car with the air conditioning on AND your windows down!

PPS: My glasses have been in style for the last twenty years. Pffffmphhhhhh.

PPPS: Who really knows what the "G.W." stands for?? Not me.

Open Letter to a Waterbug

Waterbug,

Hey little fellow. Whatcha doing way down there in this portajohn? Are ya on holiday? (Just kidding!) It looks like you are clinging onto... OH MY GOD. That is SOOOOOOOO NASTY! Ok, ewwwwwwwwwww!

Looking down into a public portajohn is one of mankind's strangest, nonsensical temptations. We know it's gonna be repulsive, yet somehow we must sate a morbid sense of curiosity by peeking into the abyss. Why do we do it? To see if maybe, just maybe, there is ONE single entry-level portajohn IN THIS WORLD that isn't absolutely disgusting? (My own personal search continues unabated.) With a hot stove, we lay our hands on it only once—the pain is too much to repeat the action. Same with looking at the sun. It is done only once. But with a portajohn, we look at the retina-burning mess each and every time and I for one, never cease to be amazed. Or repulsed. Perhaps it's the nature of man to examine, errr, the nature of man? Is there a worse thing to hear than a young daughter saying, "Daddy, I have to go number two RIGHT NOW" and seeing only a (men's) public portajohn? There may be no more abrupt loss of innocence to the uninitiated than this experience, and rhetorically speaking, there just ain't enough Purell in the universe...

I'm sorry to make light of it. This is about *you*, water skimmer. You were designed by Mother Nature to cruise happily across an open pond (*fresh* water please!) and take advantage of the physics of the universe that let the likes of you dance on water and the likes of me sink. Nature's a capricious thing, ehh? A fickle mistress, indeed. There you are going along minding your own business, then, bam! Next thing you know, you are clinging onto a turd for dear life.

Are you one of those cryptic life lessons delivered to all and ignored by most? Why have you caught my eye? Why have our paths crossed? Your message is lost on me—all I see is a ginormous Kilimanjaro of fetid, human waste. And you, a sorry cherry perched on top (to mix completely unrelated metaphors). You have gotten yourself into (maybe even **on**to?) a real pickle. And, as if being down there is not bad enough, it's a balmy 98 degrees out. Things cook and break down at that temperature. I guess you know that by now.

I'm not entirely sure I like being in *this* position either. I was just out for a run. Innocent enough, right? I decided to be polite and use this contraption instead of getting scolded by the park ranger for going on the side of the running path where all the other animals go—the idea being I might save an animal by not pissing on it in the wild. But here I am. And there you are! Ironic, huh? Where are the policy wonks when you need them?

Well, now what? A better Wally would rest his cheek carefully on the toilet seat, reach all the way down into the murky, vile depths of this uncontested, noxious hell and then, between my trembling index finger and thumb, carefully shake you off and pull you to safety. Return you to your worried family. That's what a more self-enlightened, magnanimous Wally would do. The imperfect version that I'm stuck with is not doing that, however. Not even close. And I feel bad because although the waters on which you tread are suspiciously azure and calm for the moment, they will eventually do you in.

If only... If only those chemically treated, cerulean blue waters were lapping the white beaches of Jost Van Dyke in the British Virgin Islands. And if only that turd wrapped in toilet paper you cling to was the sun-bleached, teak decks and luffing white sails of a 34' centerline ketch, burying the rail at eight knots, plying the trade winds on a broad reach with a chokingly full spinnaker. If only...

You close your little waterbug eyes and dream. Go ahead. Here's hoping some real nature lover (with a large pair of elbow-deep, latex examination gloves and a larger sense of compassion than I) comes along soon. I'm no expert, but I'm giving you a dozen minutes. Tops. Here's hoping you come back in the next life in some form that can't fit, even if it tried, into one of these portajohns (A whale? An elephant?). Seems it might be karmically appropriate to spare you another round of

106

this business of accidentally finding your way back into a toilet bowl of any size.

If I see your friends and family on the rest of my run in Minnewaska State Park, shall I tell them that you went out bravely? Put up a fight? Or shall I just lower my head and say nothing? Deny we ever met?

It's funny, if you were a cockroach down there, I'd probably take sport in dispatching you with my own biblical flood of urine. Now the urge to relieve myself (at least in this unit and at your expense) is gone. Lucky for me, there are 10 more identical units in a row right next to it. If fate were kinder, you'd have encountered my sister who travels with floss at all times. It may be floss to her, but to you, it could be a waxed and minty life rope. (Well, after she used it, but still...)

Now, I got to go (so to speak). Good luck and I hope you don't think less of me for not reaching in and saving you. I'm sure that'll cost me later (when I come back in the next life as a water bug?). Right now, I have three more miles to run.

-Wally

PS: It says this thing was cleaned just last week (!?!). So I guess things could be worse...

Got a story to share about portajohns? Or just need advice? Email Wally at cwn4@aol.com.

Wally's Guest Column in Nature Tales

The first big snow of the year is always exciting for me and today, my 60-pound pooch and I will venture out into the forest to embrace it. I like to travel with him for the sense of security—I know in a pinch, if I get lost and disoriented, and there's no sign of help for days, I can always eat him. (He's incredibly loyal!) Any port in a storm, I say. Above all, Mother Nature demands of her kin that the natural order not be held in abeyance. Harsh as it sounds, if one of us is getting burgered up, it ain't gonna be me. Shepherd pie, if resources allow. German shepherd pie, if not. Know what I mean?

As a naturalist, I like to commune with nature and all her magical incarnations. The serenity of the quiet forest is like no other drug I've ever taken. Getting into this sublime "zone" is a mental challenge at times. It can also present formidable physical challenges.

For sure you've heard of the Werner Herzog produced documentary "Grizzly Man." This steady-cam, cinema verite, selfie account follows my fellow naturalist Timothy Treadwell as he cribs up with his "brothers and sisters," the Kodiak Alaskan grizzly bears. The familial bonds, unfortunately, were not so warmly reciprocated—a 700 pound, savage "brother from another mother" turned on the interloper and yanked him out of his flimsy tent by the underwear, eating him and finally pooping him out in the shape of a steaming pile of freaked out, gig-gone-wrong scat.

Yee-owww.

The adult male bear did it because it was either hungry or bored or irritated (Tim was a little irritating, truth be told, and I feel horrible saying this because, well, before he was a piece of crap, he was a person).

There's a lesson in here somewhere for all you would-be naturalists. This profession (naturalist) is no sinecure, and it shouldn't be attempted by the under-experienced. Sure, walk to the garden and get your tomatoes. That's probably ok. The wilderness, however, is dangerous. Nature has teeth and they are friggin' sharp. Stay in your cars where it is safe and leave the deep stuff to the pros.

Like me.

I wear a fashionable Kevlar scarf in case a mountain lion pounces from a tree limb and tries to sink its fangs into my neck, which hasn't happened, but could. The Kevlar scarf is also helpful in the event of a Zombie invasion or if I get an invitation* to lunch up at the Mohonk Mountain House by a fan of this column. (Errr??)

And I keep my wildlife immersion limited to relatively harmless creatures like the Yellow-bellied Sapsucker and the noisy, Pileated Woodpecker with its proud and puffing red breast. Or crest. Or whatever it is.

I actually hate those little peckers, in particular, because they make an awful racket and disrupt the lyrical forest incantations.

The virgin season snow creates an insulated blanket that allows me and my dog to approach the woodpecker on foot without excessive fanfare.

I shuffle toward the denser woods, going deeper than is probably wise. I'm lured by the relentless staccato of the bird's beak rata-tat-tat-tatting on a punky tree trunk. I need to make the noise end.

Finally I see the pecker about 20 feet up. I've got him cornered. I get out my binoculars and pull his busy body into focus. He stops briefly to inspect me with cocked head and suitable curiosity. Then he's back at it. This is glorious!

I pull out my Daisy Air Rifle and pop off a few rounds at him until I see a poof of feathers. This finally causes the pecker to shut his bark hole and move on.

The forest briefly returns to its natural state of quiet and all is back to normal.

Job well done.

I glance around and my dog is gone. The lummox has bounded off into the milky backdrop of a passing snow squall perhaps to sniff out and politely parry with a playful squirrel.

When I catch up with him, he's found a squirrel alright. It's laying limp in his mouth like a tube sock filled with wet sand and he is looking mighty proud.

Caaaaa-Raaaaap.

The naturalist should tread lightly in Mother Nature's house. We are her guests. She's our hostess. The naturalist should refrain from unnecessary species eradication whilst out in the field. I am disappointed with my dog, and with myself frankly, for not being more present, but I give him a cookie and a pat on the head and ask him to be more careful next time.

That should do the trick.

It's time to return to civilization and say goodbye to this quiet wonderland. For now.

I've got a crockpot going at home of stewed twigs, unrecognizable red berries and ice-encrusted oak leaves which I'll serve over a nice bed of woodstove warmed lichen this evening before the explosive consequence of excessive roughage that is the occupational hazard of a good naturalist sets in.

I'm also ready to go because I'm cold. One thing about being a real naturalist that often is NOT mentioned in the paper by regular *Nature Tales* columnist Ann Guenther, is that to do the job purely, and bear this is mind as you read her fine column, it must be done completely in the nude. As nature intended...

We dress to please the hostess!

Well, that's my thing.

It's excruciatingly painful but I walk on my toes trying carefully not to crush the virgin snow on my way out of this utopia. It's not fair to the snowflakes whose individuality I have to honor. I salute this forest (Mother Nature's gift to us) from the parking lot and finish off with an extra deep, respectful, good-bye, man-curtsey.

Until, and if, we are invited back to guest-host this column, and that's a big IF, please enjoy the continued musings of my fellow naturalist, Ann, who will be back next issue when her ankle heals from getting stuck in the illegal iron jaw coyote leg trap I left out and forgot to tell her about.

My bad.

*There's a better chance of a mountain lion attack, actually.

TRADITIONS

February

Dear Wally,

I don't like February. It's dark and cold. About the only good thing I can say about it is that it is shorter than the other months. But still, it isn't short enough. Can you give me some perspective to help me get through it?

-T in Accord

Dear T,

I think I can do you one better than a new perspective. How about I actually get rid of February for you? I've been thinking about running for high office, like Governor, and I'd need a unique, hot-button campaign platform issue that hasn't been co-opted and regurgitated by the big boys on the right or the left thousands of times over like health care reform, balanced budget, bank bailouts, etc.

Removing February. Hmmmmm. It's never been promised before. This might work. I think New Yorkers might get behind me on this. Let's see how it sounds from atop a soapbox:

Fellow New Yorkers, thank you for coming out today. I want to be your governor. If you vote for me, I'll remove February. It's dark and cold. It's also short. I realize this may cost me the short vote, but to hell with them—there are a lot of tall people out there (and long months) to compensate. (By the way, to minimize the hemorrhage of short voters, I'm hereby defining "short" as under one foot tall or fewer than 29 days.)

February is also costly. Hear me out. I know it's cold and you are tired. With only 28 days, mortgages, rents, utilities and pretty much any monthly expenses are shoehorned into three fewer days and thus proportionally more expensive per day than in longer months. Further, municipalities blow most of their budget in February on plowing and salting roads. What a waste. We have nothing to show for it in June. In these days of fiscal austerity, every New Yorker could use a break. I think educated voters and burdened townships will see my logic and be supportive of removing February as a necessary cost-savings measure. People aren't stupid, people. Between the icicles hanging from my frozen beard, I smell votes.

Presidents Washington and Lincoln have February birthdays and thus will be upset. But since leaving office, their daily influence has been greatly marginalized. In short, I'm not worried about them or their attack dogs on the Sunday morning talk shows.

The Valentine's Day lobby might take it hard on the chin as they've spent a lot of money marketing mid-February. The letterhead and business cards are already printed. But everyone I know always runs out of time getting bon-bons and flowers for their sweethearts, so most of New York probably won't mind shoving the holiday back into March or April.

The average daily temperature is 34.3 degrees. As you New Yorkers know, it is extremely difficult to make ice at this temperature. Getting rid of February means getting rid of problems for this important (voting) segment of the economy. We need solutions right now, not more problems. (Insert applause here.) I know I can count on the ice makers' vote to help me.

The horoscope writers should love this proposal—it's less work for them. That means more time to spend in the markets buying things and stimulating the economy. Or more time with their families. Shorter horoscopes also mean less wasted ink and paper. That should keep the tree huggin' environmentalists happy.

Febuary is also extremely hard to spell (see?). Getting rid of it will make fourth graders around the state happier and smarter.

While it is true they don't vote, happy fourth graders make for happy parents. Happy parents make for happy votes.

Procedurally, getting rid of February will be like a calendar facelift. We make a few small incisions after Christmas and before Easter, remove February, and stretch the other months taut. We'll then suture January to March and, voila!— all the year's wrinkles are gone. We'll look 30 years younger too!

Speaking of wrinkles, I can only think of one. My daughter's birthday is in February.

And as I think on this a bit more, my dear constituency, I'm coming to the career-stopping reality that she won't like this move at all. She'll be two this year and is fully expecting a party. And what is a politician if not a family guy?

It is for this reason, and after great deliberation, that I'm sorry to announce that I will not seek the office of Governor in the interest of spending more time with my family. February will have to stay, and because my hands are cold this stump speech will have to end.

Sorry, T, but you'll have to look on the bright side of having February—the days are getting longer and warmer.

Wish I could have helped a bit more.

-Wally

Got a question for our advice columnist or just want to lobby him about making summer longer? Email him at cwn4@aol.com.

Earth Day

Dear Wally,

Earth Day is coming up. I know that we all have much to be thankful for and there's much to be gained by sharing and celebrating our commonality, though it seems a hard sell these days to culturally weave that encompassing reality into something that doesn't resemble a very flimsy g-string. Statistics and warnings and film clips of melting icebergs and polar bears clutching life rafts are losing their punch as we numb to their repetitious exposure. What do you think? I feel the world's people are scratching their paunches, ho-humming and going back to life as they know it in their corners of a flat world. Tell me we are all connected, please?

-An Earth Lover Feeling Alone

Dear Earth Lover,

With a little bit of eavesdropping, a few questions, Google, and some speculation, I'm ready to prove, once again, to those who still don't believe it, that the earth is round, and we are connected. And as my friend who knows I get lost all the time says, don't worry, you'll eventually get back where you started because the world is round. You'll meet a lot of folks on the way, but you'll get back. The earth's roundness is our connectivity, our complexity and our commonality, illustrated in part through the seemingly simplest of actions—drinking a cup of coffee.

I am in a New York coffee shop. In my hands is a hot cup of coffee. I consider the roundish shape and global implications of the bean we worship.

Ok, *I* worship.

In the corner of this small shop, which is owned by a Spaniard, are rough burlap bags of coffee beans grown in Guatemala and picked in part by Hondurans.

The 100-pound sacks are loaded onto a Japanese-designed truck which runs on diesel. This fuel comes from Venezuela and is refined in the Caribbean. The truck travels to the seaport where the beans are offloaded into a container made of Indian steel. The container is loaded onto a cargo ship which was financed by the Austrians, made in the Netherlands, captained by an Australian, crewed by Indonesians, fueled by the Saudis and registered in Panama. The ship has just arrived from Singapore by way of the Portuguese Azores and all on board are relieved to have successfully avoided Somali pirates.

The captain wears a ring that is made from the gold and diamonds of two African countries. The setting was handled by an Israeli jeweler in Istanbul. It reminds the captain of his New Zealand wife whom he misses and so calls on a Korean cell phone (which was made in China) to say he is alive and well.

The shipping manifest for the coffee bean that makes up my coffee is written on a laptop designed in the US and manufactured in Taiwan with final assembly in Mexico. A satellite with Czech avionics tracks the cargo as it makes its way north.

In America it is offloaded by enormous Norwegian cranes operated by an American-born Kenyan who smokes an illegal Cuban cigar. A heavy-duty Swedish truck with tires from Brazilian rubber takes the container to a distribution center, and it makes its way to a Vermont operation that uses natural gas from Canada to run the bean roaster.

Then it's back on a truck driven by a UPS man in a brown uniform made in Thailand and brown boots from Senegal. He drops the roasted beans off with the coffee shop's nice English manager (of Lebanese and Asian heritage) who signs for them with a pen made in Bangladesh while she serves a Russian man

Irish coffee with a hint of Madagascarian vanilla. He hopes he doesn't spill it on his Egyptian cotton shirt.

If the wood from the coffee shop's frame could talk, I'd have proof from the way it says, "Eh?", that it was milled in Quebec, even though the logs are from New Jersey.

The manager takes the beans and drops them in a French-made grinder before putting them into an Italian latte machine. She rings a small bell made in Tibet which signals that my order is up.

I take the coffee cup to my table, cup it in my hands and happen to look in the corner and—whaddya know! A few burlap bags of coffee beans from Guatemala!

As the caffeine works its way into my body, I become even more aware of a reason to celebrate.

Happy Earth Day indeed, you round world!

-Wally

Got a question for our advice columnist? Just want to argue that the earth is flat? Or yell at him because he forgot to mention Greece? Email him at cwn4@aol.com.

Halloween

Dear Wally,

Your take on Halloween?

-Don

Don,

I've given it, and my recent experience with it, some thought. Here goes:

Parents all over are forgiven for the once-a-year Fall ritual of dressing their wee toddlers up as bumble bees or pumpkins. The children are too young to feel humiliated (until the pictures resurface years later) and the "cute" payoff in the here and now is typically too enormous for us parents to resist. In the bigger scheme, except for the sugar spike the kids receive for indulging us, it's a victimless crime, right?

This was the first year that Halloween really resonated with my near three year old. Certainly its commercialization was suitably in place with stores featuring ghoolies, mountains of orange candy, pumpkins and fake tombstones. It would be impossible for anyone three or older to not notice weeks in advance that Halloween, or at least some strange event, was bearing down on us like a runaway freight train.

We bought into it fully for her, and for us, and were actually quite excited to dust off the abandoned practice of trick-or-treating, which I had given up at 14 after having been more exposed to the trick part than the treat part. (I had been out for candy that night but instead got caught up in a dark mix of rotten eggs, shaving cream and Nair hair removal. But that was years ago and the innocent part of the holiday has cycled back, fortunately.)

My young daughter was just not sure about the big picture of knocking on a stranger's door, saying a few words, and getting candy. In her defense, it is a bit strange, especially as one gets to do this only one night a year. So together we ran through the paces in advance. For a few weeks before, here and there, she would practice knocking on an inside door of our house, like a closet or bathroom door, and I, crouched on the other side, would pretend to be the treat-wielding homeowner.

At first, she would knock on the door and say with great enthusiasm, "Candy!" which is what she really wanted. But with a little help and scripting from me, we soon unlearned the abrupt "Candy!" line and got the right one down. First, knock knock knock. Then, "Trick or treat!"

I even suggested that a typical homeowner might ask her what she is dressed as and she might want to tell them. After this exchange, she might receive a piece of candy. I neglected to tell her that some folks might instead offer her a juicy apple from one of the local orchards. I didn't bother telling her this because those houses are usually quickly identified by kids and avoided as if haunted. My own house growing up was just such a house and my mother always wondered why no one showed up for her apples or raisins. Of course it takes being so old that you can't fit one leg in a size 4T monkey costume to realize that a one-dollar apple is the better bargain all the way around and that having just such an apple-giving mother is not mortifying, but in fact cool. Ah, youth.

Anyway, I told Hattie that she might also warm up the homeowner with a few pleasantries to dilute the "gimme" feel, and that this might possibly increase the overall candy haul. For example, "Wow mister, look at all that firewood you chopped—you must be strong," or "What a lovely shade of semi-gloss buttermilk white you have chosen as a window trim color."

And however she decided to handle herself, she was to look them in the eye and say, "Thank you," and not leave the shreds of her candy wrapper on their lawn as she departed.

She had trouble deciding what she wanted to be. Those with the most purchase in days prior were: A witch, a huge cardboard pumpkin (my secret favorite) and an Elmo. She was fickle and inconclusive and she bandied, as was and will hopefully always be, her prerogative. I knew that my costume would thus be a composite of the scraps of the unused options. And indeed, night of, bright red Elmo with the bug eyes won out at the last minute, which was fine by me because it was furry and kept her warm-ish. My slapdash costume, a PumpkinWitch(!?!) was cold and confusing and I think I accidentally poked out a few eyes.

Halloween was a near perfect experience—Hattie was wide-eyed and enthusiastic and happy and amped up on the few candy bars we were not able to slip out of her bucket. She charmed and politely collected and did her thing without a single mention of house paint or woodpiles.

So how did our scripting and enthusiasm for Halloween finally play out?

A few days later, as she and I are moving through JFK International Airport, I dip into the men's room with her. As I dry my hands with a paper towel and watch her like a hawk, she bolts up to a closed bathroom stall where, as my grandmother euphemistically said, "The king goes alone." Hattie looks at the tile floor under the door and sees pants bunched up around the two wingtip shoes of a perfect stranger. Before I can stop her, she raises her hand to the bathroom stall door and knocks. What does she say? Exactly what she's practiced, "Trick or Treat!"

-Wally

Got a question for our advice columnist or just need him to dress in a tutu and be the Candy Faerie that swaps out your Halloween candy for a pet rock? Email him at cwn4@aol.com.

Host Mother

Dear Wally,

We have a foreign exchange student here for the summer (only) and she's trying to understand the rules of when to use catsup and when to use mustard. She's now attended plenty of backyard picnics but still is confused. I caught her putting mustard on a hamburger and had to reprimand her. That's what made me reach out to you, as I'm out of other options. Unbelievably, there's nothing on Google or Wikipedia about this. Can you speak to the unspoken protocol of what condiment to use when?

-Host Mother

Dear Host,

And it is an unspoken protocol, isn't it? When Google walks away from it, you really know you are pacing a lonely planet. Thanks for giving me the chance to set the record straight, once and for all.

You reprimanded a kid for using the wrong condiment? What the hell is wrong with you? Do you know what some kids today are doing? Ehhhh, nevermind.

Anyway, let me consult Miss Mary Manners' Clever Condiment Conduct Handbook so your guest can not only enjoy her American food more, but she can take our ways back to the dirt-road heathens with whom she lives and cavorts, and in so doing expand the US culinary hegemony, one loaded jumbo hot dog at a time. She can be one part wide-eyed cultural attaché and one part condiment proselytizer if we do this right. Onward and upward! Mayofest Destiny.

In any event, it's part of her cultural study here so if she's gonna learn (and then teach?) our ways, she ought to at least learn the right ones.

I've studied the relationship between condiments and food extensively (thought about doing a dissertation on it but couldn't get into a grad school I liked that also had a coed Ultimate Frisbee team so I bailed. No point in playing that silly game with just dudes). And there's no better time to explore the do's and don'ts of these dominant, heavy-weights (catsup and mustard) than summertime which is when we carry them to BBQs pretty much like six-shooters in holsters at our sides. And which is now.

This is why I have moved this question to the very top of the slush pile of letters seeking advice. (You, the guy with the compound femur fracture who wrote in seeking advice about which ER department is best and nearest? You will have to wait another week.) This week it's about condiments because... before we know it, the summer BBQ season will have slipped away and your exchange student will be left scratching her head at JFK Departures wondering what in the hell just happened, and more importantly, what she needs to do now.

I'm under great pressure these days (time, space, money, diminishing fresh air and now shortening daylight) so forgive me for "teaching to the test," as it were. There ARE some basic no-no's that I'll try to articulate in the context of laying out the complicated, love-hate relationship between catsup and mustard—a relationship that is fraught with nuance, control, resentment, jealousy, rivalry and often, issues of abandonment. (I'm no therapist, but I spend enough time with them...) In really bad cases, the two can turn violent (usually warring in your GI track for a few tense hours).

I've come to frame certain foods as merely subjugated vehicles for one or the other of these major condiments, and that's probably a function of me being pretty damn American. Catsup's in my blood.

Can't eat the stuff straight up. That's pretty much rule number one. Doing so is revolting for even the biggest fan. That said, ALMOST eating it straight up seems to be just fine. Grilled cheeses, for example, stripped to the chassis of just bread and cheese, leap to another culinary platform altogether when dipped in catsup, or better yet, submerged in catsup. But you wouldn't dare put mustard on a grilled cheese now would you? This monumental culinary gaff would be akin to pouring mustard into a Gin and Tonic. Or, egads, mustard on a hamburger—an action as you well know that can break up a party pretty quickly and bring large-scale shame upon your house.

Cold cheese sandwiches, however, (ungrilled, that is) should not have catsup whatsoever. Make note. That is totally gross. Same core ingredients (bread and cheese) but the experience is RUINED by sullying an ungrilled cheese sandwich with catsup. Mustard on it is perfect. Figure THAT out, foreigners!

Catsup on fries? Certainly. It's actually wrong to NOT put catsup on fries. Other cultures put mayonnaise, mustard and vinegar on their fries. But other cultures are wrong.

Catsup on an egg and cheese sandwich? You betcha. Catsup on just eggs? Puke me out. Not happening.

What a razor thin line! How can anyone make sense of these cultural nuances? It's a small miracle that even American-born eaters are able to keep it all straight.

Where it all comes together though, and where fragile peace is finally forged, is atop the almighty American hot dog. Here, there are no rules and everything gets along. Catsup complements mustard in a way that otherwise never happens. There's no top billing and no bitterness (even with horseradish mustard). Condiment egos are marginalized for the greater good of the eater's experience. Everything and any combo works up there.

The hot dog, then, becomes the macro metaphor for America herself; a backbone upon which a melting pot of influences and tastes as represented by the colorful, tasty and complimentary medley of condiments, is saddled in perfect harmony between the bun's protective walls, which for this example we can call the mighty East and West coasts.

Plus a loaded hotdog tastes great.

Burp.

Good luck and check your exchange student's pockets for the family silver before she leaves.

-Wally

Got a question for our advice columnist, or an extra *au pair* kicking around? Email him at cwn4@ol.com.

Catching Up with Goldilocks:

A Special Edition Dear Wally

When the discussion of food in literature arises in the circles of the intelligentsia, noses turn upward to the likes of Sylvia Plath, who not only artfully nuanced food with her pen but who also actually tried to cook her own head.

Let's take it down a peg and remember the archetypical literary muncher whose fickle palette brought unto her a house of un-bear-able (ahem) pain and suffering in the first place, and sparked the modern day food-in-literature movement. I'm talking about the cutest curly blond interloper out there without a formal criminal record.

I caught up with Goldilocks recently and the former child star was gracious enough to give me some time. I told her I was doing a piece on food in literature for my *BlueStone Press* column.

She now runs a Korean taco cart in Kingston. Her fortunes have turned more times than the seasons since her childhood immortalization in print. She's been in all the chic rehabs and on all the late-night TV couches. Her postered likeness has graced every nursery and every cinder block college dorm wall.

She's come a long way from the smeared mascara, ripped stockings and handcuffs the tabloids used to delight in.

She's quiet and introspective now—the marks of wizened maturity from someone who started out on a path of crime. She explains that fateful day:

"My parents were freakin' hippies in leafy tunics and went off chasing wood faeries one day when we were camping somewhere on Route 28 west of Woodstock. I got bored in the RV and started exploring. Before I knew it I was lost. All those damn trees look the same! This is pre-GPS, mind you, or my life would have been radically different."

She interrupts herself without missing a beat and tends to a waiting customer.

"Hey mister, you want extra hot sauce with that taco?"

The gritty sounds of survival buck me out of her dreamy narrative. But then she's back and I'm right there with her.

"So, after wandering, I got hungry. I guess food has always been my weakness," she confesses, licking imaginary BBQ sauce off her fingertips.

"My parents told me not to eat wild berries or I'd get, like, wicked diarrhea. I observed *that* rule so they get points for that. But they lose points for flaking out and forgetting to tell me about breaking and entering."

I can see from the way she moves the hissing meat scraps around the taco grill that the passion for food is still there. And a little bit of the anger too.

"We're all good now—my parents, the bears, me. Look, it was wrong to break into their house. I get that.

"I've done a lot of inner work, and well, I wouldn't do it again… Everyone has a right to privacy."

I ask the painful question that has to be asked: "Was the porridge good?"

It was, after all, the foundation of her infamy.

She looks up at the sky and I swear I see a tear. Could be the sizzling onions. Could also be the sizzling truth.

"Wally," she whispers leaning in, clutching my collar and choking up just a little bit, "The baby bear's was the best flippin' hot cereal I've ever had. Illegally good.

"The poppa bear's was too hot, for sure. But what they left out of the book, and maybe it'll make it into the movie if they ever do it, is that the poppa bear's porridge also tasted horrible. No one could have eaten it. That's why he stormed out.

"What about the mother's porridge?" I ask delicately. "Too cold?"

She goes all wide-eyed. "It was spiked with schnapps."

"Noooooooooooo!!!" I scream.

"Yeah, they left that part out too. But even that little taste made me woozy. That's why I went upstairs—to sleep it off.

"For a long time people thought I was rifling through the bear's underwear drawer like some sicko. Wanna know something?"

I lean in.

"Bear don't wear underwear."

I lean back out.

"I just wanted to bed off the schnapps. Simple as that. I'm really glad I could get that off my chest after all these years.

"Well what now?" I ask, looking at the bleak commercial prospects of running a taco cart in one's late middle age and trying to be polite.

"Well, I'm starting a line of boutique instant porridge. I've come pretty darn close to recreating the stuff I had that day in the woods. Only this has Omega 3s and Omega 6s, and is fortified with organic chestnuts, sea krill and Himalayan salt. Oh, and then low-heat simmered in a raw Afghan goat milk reduction sauce before being flash frozen in a BPA-free microwaveable pouch. It's gonna be big. Whole Foods is already in."

And here I was thinking Goldilocks was two dimensional. (She still is paper thin by the way.)

Then she turns to me, looks at the watch I got for graduation, and I brace for what I know is coming.

"I need another $50,000 in start-up money," she sighs. "I've already sold the literary rights to my comeback story and burned through the cash.

"But," she adds, poking a spatula at my solar plexus, "I've got a solid business plan and I'm an established brand. You think any of those *BlueStone Press* readers might want to invest?"

Got a question about politics or life or love or economics? Or have you spotted a former child star living locally whose follow up story simply needs to be told? Email our advice columnist at cwn4@aol.com.

RELATIONSHIPS

Rules of Dating

Dear Wally,

I've recently started seeing someone and it's going well. She's fun, smart, and cute, and knows how to drive a stick-shift pickup truck. She has nice fingernails and she even smells great. It's been going so well in fact that I'm starting to get concerned. We haven't had a fight, or even a disagreement in the month we've known each other. Should I be nervous?

-JR

Dear JR,

Ahhh, JR, finally a good old fashioned, Cold War era, *Dear Abby*-esque relationship question. Thank YOU! I don't even think that old battle axe Abby Landers (Ann Landers? If there's even a difference??) is still around, but either way, I'm sure she'd approve of me fielding your concerns thusly:

Let me crack my knuckles and get right to this refreshing question. No fights yet? What is wrong with you? Fix that. You are really mishandling this one, friend. Shape up and foment some relationship drama, stat. If you are not lucky enough to be bickering like a pair of Boston fish wives already, you'll have to make your own luck and initiate some conflict.

Why?

To understand and appreciate a positively trending dynamic, you have to explore its opposite. Early on, while you both smell good to each other, (and that will change, son) you need to know how a partner will fight, when or if the BIG ONE comes. Apparently you have been deprived of this experiential data.

So to tease this relationship dynamic out, make sure you do something really stupid, right now, just so you can see the rules of engagement. You are only a month into this inchoate relationship, what with its "new car" smell and all, so there still is time, but I caution you, not much.

Suggestions follow, realizing that a good pissing-off usually precipitates the exact conflict you need, however disingenuous or engineered or prickly (or final?) it may be.

So, anyhoo, here ya go:

Finish off the ice cream and leave the empty container on its side in the fridge (not the freezer). Borrow a friend's bra and shove it down under the covers (you better have hockey padding on for this one). Run the car out of gas (hers!). Intentionally park as far away in the movie theater parking lot as possible (this is a failsafe fight starter). The list of possible obnoxious antics is long, but remember, you are doing it FOR LOVE and because you believe in the long-term viability of the relationship!

To be comprehensive though, you might want to also consider the following, which flies directly in the face of what has been driveled out above: I know you are skeptical of conflict-free love, but is it possible that this budding relationship is just plain and simply... fine? Maybe you are looking for trouble unnecessarily? True, you are in the honeymoon phase, and suitably doe-eyed by the compendium of pulchritude with which you shellac your mate (nice fingernails? Really? Who says that?) but it could just be as simple as having the right mate. Imagine that?

I don't want to scare you with this notion. Just letting it waft out there on the currents a bit...

A cautionary note: For an advice columnist, I am disturbingly under-qualified to advise on relationships, at least in any academic capacity. I've much to say anecdotally—had my spleen punctured by a date's stiletto (don't ask)—but that and the fact that I'm stepping through the detritus of all my past relationships, yes, all that and $2.25 will get you on the New York City subway. Just bear that in mind. (Maybe it's gone up from $2.25, too. Best check on that…)

I took one single Psychology class in college, from which I chiefly remember just two things: 1) studying Rorschach blots with typical freshman male zeal ("uhhh, these ALL look like boobs?!?") (Luckily in Psych 101 there's no wrong answer, even when you actually DO give a wrong answer) and 2) I remember training rats to smack levers for feed pellets, which led me to believe that if this whole college thing didn't work out, I knew at least I could train albino, caged rats to hit a lever and get food. And if THAT specialized vocational skill set also didn't work out, or the global market for pellet-smackin' rat trainers dried up somehow, and I couldn't get any other job, and I started going hungry, at least I knew I could eat rat pellets. And when the pellets run out, eat rats. So at least I wouldn't starve. (One tends to think about this logic chain when one is splayed on a beanbag chair in a freshman dorm listening to *Pink Floyd*.)

In Psych 101, we didn't spend much time "in the mind" as it were. Maybe if I didn't go flitting from the Psychology Department to the English Department the moment the Freudian penis-talk was whipped out (so to speak), I'd be better prepared for your dilemma.

So much for my bona-fides… Like I said, punctured spleen and $2.25!

Well, good luck with this JR, and I'm serious about the hockey padding if you use the bra gag…

-Wally

Got a question for our advice columnist or just have cracked, protective hockey gear you are no longer using (because you are single)? Email him at cwn4@aol.com.

Geek Squad

Dear Wally,

My computer just died. Help!

-Distraught

Dear Distraught,

Let me share a recent personal diary entry that might help:

Dear Geek Squad,

I'll never make fun of you again if you can get my computer to turn on. Last night while I was working, it died on me. Bam. Gone. Black screen. No warnings, no apologies. I tried smacking, rebooting, yelling, and then I tried beer. I went through Kubler-Ross's five stages of grief and now I'm at acceptance. Except I'm not really because I cling to a sliver of hope: You.

Today I'm at your formica counter, hat in hand. I am biting my tongue for all the snotty, mean things I could easily say about your skinny black tie and greasy hair (and thick glasses held together by electrical tape, tucked in shirt, shiny shoes, Sears "Toughskins" black slacks and knowing smug smile)—the way you ride the back of the consumer electronics giant BestBuy like a sycophantic, scrap-nibbling remora—things I usually say behind your back.

I will say none of these things because right now, I am your bee-atch. But I'll go one further: If you retrieve my data (some of which includes an essay making fun of you), I'll never ever again make fun of ANYONE in the tech customer support business, no matter how homely they are, no matter how much they look like they are guiding Apollo 13 to the moon from Houston fifty years too late.

Make this deal with me now, and your cousins at Verizon who delight in flummoxing me and your cable TV brethren who revel in tardiness (and who never have the right part in their truck) will all be safe from my invective from here on out. So long as you hook up your gizmo and breathe life back into my computer, I'll do you that solid and you will know that at least one voice in a mocking sea of gazillions has been silenced. Ok? Be a hero to your people.

Take my computer and caress it with your magic hands on that static-proof bench over there while I fidget nervously. Admire its ram or gigs. Have your way with it. My life is in your hands. My entire past and my entire future.

You behind that counter. Me at your mercy. It's a dynamic I do not enjoy. I damn everyone in your profession under my breath. I nervously look at the clock and then the rate card ($95 per hour) and then the clock again. You decide that it's sloth time and that revenge, while best served cold, is also a dish best served slowly (at $95 per hour). On the clock, you admire the bag I brought the laptop in—the same bag the BestBuy "hostess" thinks I'm gonna use to steal small consumer electronics. I shift my weight uneasily, trying to tell you with body language that the "fix," if there is one, is not with my leather bag.

I feel my life savings run through the sieve of your skinny, Darwinian-advanced, capacitor-gripping fingers. There goes this month's rent! We sail past the unspoken initial, free ten-minute rule, wherein, if you Geek Squaders can fix it, there's no charge. No sir, that won't be my fate.

I'm doomed.

Soon I'll own a useless $450 laptop that cost me $5,000 to not fix.

"No boot device, you say?" My words sound hollow. "What's that mean? Is that good or bad?"

"Wait… either very good or very bad? I think I need to throw up."

You point over your shoulder at the black curtain that shields the secret room and tell me you are going to have to "take it in the back."

"Well that makes two of us," I joke.

No smiles.

You, wizard, step slowly ($95 per hour) backward and disappear, mumbling the words, "I'll be right back." The black curtain swallows you up. A loved one off to the operating room. I pace the cold tiles.

I have time.

I find myself drifting toward the beeping, clanging lure of new equipment that flanks me in the enormous store. Somehow I arrive, unawares, at the new laptop section. Is this chance? Infidelity? I doubt I'm anything other than a pawn in this heady game. I've follow the carpeted path that the plump statisticians and marketing cerebrums have conjured.

And then I hear your voice float over the store. You hold my laptop open, splayed casually yet firmly (like the unfortunate frog that we dissected in sixth grade that was pinned to a wax bed) in one arm. I see the familiar cerulean blue desktop. My palm tree, escapism screensaver sways. I see my past, my future. It's so beautiful I could cry.

Come to Poppa!

"How much am I in for?" I ask, garishly trolling the commercial. I need to immediately buoy the bad with the good.

"No charge."

"What? No charge? Mock me not Super Geek or I'll set a Level 7 Gorgon on you…"

"It was an easy fix. Just needed to relocate the hard drive. You got lucky, pal."

"I… I love you. No, I'm serious. I LOVE YOU. And I will never make fun of Geek Squaders again. Never!"

So he says, "Well, make sure next time you remember to back up."

And I get one last one in, because I can't help it: "You mean back up in my dorky little black and white VW bug mobile-service-pod?" (Hee hee.)

So, Distraught, get to BestBuy and find the Geek Squad counter. (They have the skinny black ties and thick glasses). And keep your fingers crossed!

-AllyWa

(Pig Latin code for me, in case I ever need to use Geek Squad again!)

Need a question answered, or someone to take your laptop to Geek Squad? Email our advice columnist at cwn4@aol.com.

Twinkie and Carrot

A one-act, action-less play obliquely about healthy choices, employing *deus ex machina*, a big playwriting no-no, and fake boobs, an even bigger playwriting no-no.

Dramatis Personae:

Twinkie (Tubularly rotund. Abrupt in nature.)

Carrot (Ectomorph-ish, with a floppy shock of unwieldy, green hair. Ray-Ban sunglasses.)

ACT 1

Poolside. LA. Day. Beautiful people lounge everywhere.

CARROT is clearing the pool of tanning butter slicks and throttled snarls of wind-strewn coconut hair with a long-handled skimmer. His moves are fluid and deliberate. His body is taut, extruded and whippet-thin. He is sunburned to the point of being almost orange. Think Oompa Loompa.

TWINKIE is wearing an inappropriately snug, brightly colored, full-bodied plastic track suit which resembles a wrapper. He lays supine and bloated on a pool deck recliner and watches Carrot work. Twinkie uses a folded *Style* magazine (Kardashians on the cover!) to shield his eyes from the bright sun.

He steals a glance at two incredibly attractive women sunbathing across the pool from them. Twinkie mops his profusely sweating chocolate brow, trains his glance menacingly at Carrot, then finally:

Twinkie:
Carrot, you suck.
Carrot:
Excuse me??
Twinkie:
Those two over there would come over and have their way with me but that green... *thing* on the top of your head you call hair is scaring them off. Can't you dye that stuff blond? We're in LA. Be cool man. Jesus.
Carrot:
That's right, we're in LA. Where they like healthy things. Like carrots.
Twinkie:
You are delusional my orange-hued friend. Look. She's looking at me!! Look, look! She's licking her lips.
Carrot:
People believe what they want.

Twinkie:

You don't taste good. You are hard to chew. Unpleasant to the taste buds. You are the problem here, not me. Now jump in that pool and wash the peasant dirt off you.

Carrot:

Twinkie, why the hostility, you girthy sugar log?? I thought we came here to have fun. To relax.

Twinkie:

Don't call me "sugar log." Look, I get really excited, really fast. I can't help it. It's a bio-chemical imbalance.

Carrot:

Sorry.

Twinkie:

I actually don't think you are.

Carrot:

(rests on the submerged skimmer handle, then calmly)

Are we gonna get into it? Here? In front all these people? Really?

Twinkie:

(sits up and removes sunglasses)

What's THAT supposed to mean?

Carrot:

Oh, I think you know. I... I'm just going to come out and say it. You are not treating yourself with respect. Look at you. You've let yourself go. You look like... *a Twinkie.* How am I supposed to respect you if you don't even respect yourself?

Twinkie:

I am lovable. I am kind. I bring pleasure to people. I taste *fine* and I am who I am.

Carrot:

Yes. (pause) Twinkie?

Twinkie:

Yes, Carrot? What do you want? To apologize?

Carrot:

Do you feel good after you eat you?

Twinkie:

I feel great, thank you. Energized. Alive.

Carrot:
And then?

Twinkie:
And then... (long pause)... I feel crappy. (bitterly) There, I said it. Are you happy now?

Carrot:
Your pain doesn't give me pleasure. When you hurt, I hurt. (another long pause) Twinkie?

Twinkie:
Yes?

Carrot:
Do you resent that I have no ingredients?

Twinkie:
Do you resent that I have 248 and none of them are naturally occurring?

Carrot:
I don't know. No. Maybe a little. Twinkie?

Twinkie:
Yes?

Carrot:
Do you sleep naked?

Twinkie:
What the hell kind of question is that? Are you getting weird on me? It happens that I prefer track suits. (Twinkie presses down the folds of his wrapper with his palms.) Plastic ones.

Carrot:
Well it's really nice to sleep naked. In the dirt.

Twinkie:
You think because you are natural that you are somehow better than the rest of us.

Carrot:
I somehow *AM*.

Twinkie:
See? You are smug. Well, they like me better.

Carrot:
(cocking his eyebrow and nodding at the ladies). They *DO*?

Twinkie:
Well, I go into more lunchboxes than you. Kids love me. They hate you. And that's a fact. I have my own shelf in the supermarket. I can stay fresh for decades. You are a chore.
Carrot:
You sound defensive. And I am not a chore. I am a sophisticated treat. Crudite. That's French for fancy. This is about good choices.
Twinkie:
Screw you. You wilt and mold over there in the produce department with the rest of your fair-weather friends.
Carrot:
That's a low blow. We're perishable. And we're sensitive. Can you respect that?
Twinkie:
Well, you asked for it.
Carrot:
That's largely true. "Fresh for decades" is a contradiction in terms.
Twinkie:
Don't get clever with me. When people dream, they see me, not you.
Carrot:
When they wake and open their eyes, they GET to see... because of me (a long, awkward pause). Anyway, is this a contest?
Twinkie:
Whatever.
Carrot:
Fine.
Twinkie:
Fine.
Carrot:
Fine.
Twinkie:
I have other skills you know, besides just being yummy and edible. I bet you don't even know that about me.

Carrot:
I don't believe I've ever thought to ask. I am sorry. What else can you do?
Twinkie:
If I stand on one foot and hold my hand up like…

Just then a huge hand reaches down and grabs Twinkie. In a flash he is gone. There is nothing left but a discarded wrapper.

Carrot scratches the nape of his neck momentarily. Then he continues skimming the pool and pushes away what might be a tear. It also might just be a drop of sweat.

The End

Mr. Wally

June 2

Dear Mr. Wally,

God has blessed me with an honest and intelligent partner in you, my brother. Will need your legal name and credit card number and you security social number (nine digits if you are US citizen). As I am the deceased lawyer for the wealthy from oil, royal Phillip Cornell of Lome, Togo, Africa we can now start the process of getting you large inheritance ($10.5 million US) of which I take 65 percent and you take 45 percent. I urgently await your reply and also need place of birth and mother's maiden name for to send you a condolence card in case she is dead.

-Tobea Masku, Esq

Dear Tobea,

(May I call you Tobea? I feel like we can trust each other like brothers.) I respectfully must decline your generous offer for 45 percent of the $10.5 million. By the way, 45 percent plus 65 percent equals 110 percent which is even better than 100 percent! Thank you, good sir! You are indeed generous!

I am afraid I have no place to park all the Porsches I would buy. Nor would I be able to keep a 200' yacht in my small Kerhonkson farm house.

I also am concerned about what an unfathomable amount of wealth might do to my head. I thus wish to avoid the temptations of such largess and only hope it doesn't disrespect the honor of my dear, late uncle (?) Phillip Cornell. I would like to offer my services, however, for your noble cause.

I believe that you might more efficiently find the late Phillip Cornell's *next* next-of-kin via bulk email if your future written correspondence is grammatically correct.

So, I offer this proposal with the utmost respect and humility: I will proofread your correspondence at the "friends and family" rate of $100 per hour for a minimum of five hours, my brother. This would be a fine and solid investment of time and money on your part. In exchange, you will end up with a letter that you can know will not make anyone question your otherwise sterling legal credentials and bona fides (and literacy). I can start immediately.

-Wally (ummm, that's Mr. Wally, I guess)

PS: You write extremely well for a deceased lawyer!

June 3

Dear Mr. Wally,

As brothers, we should be able to open honestly against one each. I feel you are having my best interest in mind and I would be willing to increase your percentage from 45 percent to 40 percent of $10.5 million US dollars in exchange for said proofread correction. I writes Englihs better then I speak it. Dutch to. 40 percent much better then $500, yes?

Can we make a deal? I will need your security social number as well as bank routing number to receive funds from your account.

-Tobea Masku, Esq.

My Dear Tobea,

Hmmmmm. I do not seek any percentage of your $10.5 million (US dollars), even if it is an increase from 45 percent to 40 percent (!?!). I would prefer to simply take my humble fee and leave my generous share of the inheritance to you so that YOU may purchase lovely things for your family.

If you just send $500 to my PayPal account, listed below, I will happily and thoroughly start in on the five-hour project of giving you the tools you need to do your difficult job.

-Mr. Wally

PS: "Englihs" is spelled "English." This is a freebee, no-charge tip just to show you that you are in good hands!

June 4

Mr. Wally,

We play a game of cat and mouse. I am trying to offer you large monkeys. Let us not eat small raw crayfish anymore. Take my sincere offer. I am a respectable businessman and wish only the best for you and lots of ingheritence from your loving Uncle Phillip Cornell, deceased, from the diamond money.

-Tobea Maskuku, Esq.

Dear Tobea,

Wait, now diamonds? I thought we were rich on oil?!?

Crayfish are best cooked, I agree. (I think). Please let me help you help yourself. I offer a very fair and legitimate service. You will not be sorry!

-Mr. Wally

June 5

Dear Mr. Wally,

You are tire me out with your many letters. I need to make this transaction happen now for the corrupt government claims the money back and soon none is left! Please, as my brother, give the information I request so we can get you your money in certified cheque.

-Tobea Masku, Esq.

Dear Tobias,

With heavy heart, I must end this email relationship. (Plus I have to get back to work.) Sometimes it takes a sharp hook to catch a crayfish. You will have trouble catching anything but discarded tires with your mistake-filled letter.

-Mr. Wally

PS: As my brother, you should already know my (our!) mother's maiden name. No condolence card necessary as she passed away 13 years ago. Remember?

Got a question for our advice columnist or just need someone to grind down an email scammer? Contact him at cwn4@aol.com and remember, 45 percent plus 65 percent equals 110 percent, which is 10 percent more than the most possible! (This was a real email exchange by the way.)

Father Knows Best?

In response to a Letter to the Editor:

It's rare that I respond to a Letter to the Editor, but I couldn't let last issue's offering from Pastor Arnold, "Gay Marriage Sends Wrong Message," go unchecked. I'm shocked to see such an unsupportive perspective on gay marriage come forth on these *BlueStone Press* editorial pages from a fellow who knows firsthand how much damage repressive societies inflict on their citizens. To suggest, as he does, that what's happening here in America regarding gay marriage "propaganda" is what happened in the Nazi Germany he narrowly escaped is really outlandish. Just surviving that very dark era should be enough to make him and everyone cherish all humans regardless of sexual orientation. I guess the lesson was forgotten already?? Dang, that didn't take long.

Pastor Arnold says he fears that the lie of propaganda (presumably that gay marriage is ok) will eventually become accepted as truth if repeated enough. Too late! Many state legislators, some of whom are God-fearing and most of whom at least nominally represent the will of the citizens, have already accepted it as the truth. It's not just now in these spiraling days of hedonism, either—there have been gays since the cavemen days (gay + cavemen = gaveman?). Who else would have come up with the Sabertooth tiger skin summer sash and matching (tar) poolside chiffon wrap??

Meanwhile, the notion that gay marriage is against God's will has cemented pretty well with some and has been accepted by them as God's truth because they read it in a book repeatedly and now believe it. Truth through repetition. Right. So why is one propaganda truthier than another??

Why wouldn't God be extraordinarily happy that at least two of his flock are not out there killing each other for once? (He is forever stamping out that brush fire.) Moreover, why wouldn't He be beside himself with jubilation that two of his flock have instead found love and learned to cherish and support each other? It is incidental that both those members of his flock are ewes. Is it ok for rams to fight each other to death but not love each other to death?

Consider the alternative to gay marriage for those who happen to be gay—a life without socially accepted love or intimate companionship (never mind the legal rights). That's a harsh punishment! It is a deprivation of the human experience, which is, at the end of the day, all we have, and it damn well includes the right to love and be loved. Wait… doesn't institutionally denying that sound a little repressive? Remind you of anything from your past, Pastor?

Gays love raisins and put them on everything. Plus they make great parents. They can love and support and encourage kids as well as anyone. They cry real tears and bleed red blood, too. They also pay taxes and volunteer. And get this, Pastors everywhere: Statistically, gays are already part of your own congregations! Look around see if you can find them.

Is this rigid stance against gay marriage something members of the community, men and women of the cloth and ambassadors of God's love, really feel is ok policy to force on people who are gay not because it's fun, but instead because it's just the way they are? Whose god would be that intolerant? What squeaky messenger wouldn't at least question that message? Is it not time to consider softening an interpretation of the Operator's Manual that was written such a long time ago? And in so doing exercise a little human compassion? Sadly, intolerance has quite a shelf life—longer, I'm afraid, than our own journey from ashes to ashes.

Pastor, you are right that prayer for our children is in order. Ask the Catholic church's lawyers and insurance companies exactly whose behavior is "confusing" the young boys and girls today…

I recently explained to my three-year-old that Dylan has two mommies. You know what she said? "Oh. What's for lunch?" Confused? Yes, but not as confused as you, apparently.

I saw a great billboard in New York City. It said, "Don't like gay marriage? Then don't get gay married."

Someone pass me a Slurpy. And hold the raisins.

-Wally

(cwn4@aol.com)

PS: I am glad you have exercised your right to articulate your perspective. Debate on matters of opinion, however, is pointless, Pastor Arnold. Let's settle this like real men and wrestle it out naked in a vat of slippery lime Jell-O!

Oh, one last thing—I am a heterosexual minister too. With great honor and joy, I have married, and will continue to marry, happy, loving couples.

146

Dumping an Old Friend

Dear Wally,

I am getting rid of my car and I'm starting to get a little emotional about it. It has been a loyal member of the family. Yet here I am just kicking it to the curb. Should I feel bad? (I do.) Or should I just get over it and if so, how?

-Confused and Emotionally Vulnerable in Olivebridge

Dear Confused,

I think you are right to be conflicted. I do not specialize in auto-attachment grief counseling, but I know how you feel. We form attachments to inanimate objects (who never had a favorite stuffed animal?) and that's part of the human condition. I'd say it's what separates us from the monkeys, but I think if they had cars, they'd be equally remorseful when they surrendered them to the viney jungle growth. These feelings you are having mean you have compassion and empathy—and that's a good thing. If you can fall in love with a steel fender then trust me, the world would be a better place with more people like you.

My own mother, for example, used to put aspirin in the gas tank when her car backfired. She'd also smear Neosporin on the hood's rust spots. That's love. (I think.) If you actually end up giving your car a name, assigning a gender and such, the relationship will always end in heartbreak. Except for those freaks who drive their VW Bugs 1.2 million miles, we tend to outlive our cars, as we do our parents once and our pets many times over. In this way, it's a lifetime of set-ups for loss, but, happily, only after a fecund run of big love.

I recently sold my car because it had 170k miles and the heater wasn't working (to list just one of several multi-thousand-dollar fixes that wouldn't be happening on my shift). I sold it to a used-car dealer in Florida where they don't care about the heaters. I felt a pang of seller's remorse. This car had been reliable and safe—it carried my newborn daughter for the first time and countless tons of lumber. It then carried itself on the 1,500-mile Bataan Death March (AKA Route 95 south) to its own grave, as far as I was concerned. Like Moose, my once bounding, then aged, rabbit-chasing, loyal, yellow lab that has no idea that he will soon be taken on a one-way trip to the vet. (Don't worry, Moose, they have lots of rabbits in Heaven…).

I stripped the car of every last personal artifact that final day in the sunny car-dealer parking lot and it felt like a cheap, rushed exit for parting, eight-year-long friends. It was sad like *The Giving Tree* and *Cat's in the Cradle* is sad. As my buddy said earlier, those car seats have a lot of you in them, and not just the smell. Lots of good times.

Cars are not just vehicles for people, they are vehicles for memories and dreams, which if you care to allow them, can be precious things. Just as they can be, if you are neither careful nor lucky, fragile and fleeting. They mark the quick passage of time, which for the sensitive, is never reconciled without a few tears.

I'll confess I was a little misty-eyed as I looked at it proudly waiting for me to change my mind, get back in, drive away, and write the scary experience off as a one-time moment of weak indiscretion—a regretful Michael Jacksonian balcony dangle. That transactional retreat didn't happen, of course. And to the yawning, unamused used car dealer with a heavy gold neck medallion and waning patience for the likes of me, dozens of deals like this happen each day. There simply is no room for sentimental poofs in the car business.

We tend to get attached to things (and people) that help define us, just as we get attached to ourselves and our mannerisms. I don't mean in a narcissistic way, but in a grounding, channel-marking kind of way. This connection happens most prominently with family members and school friends and summer camp friends, etc. They are a prism into our own being and they tag clicks in ink along our personal, spiritual timelines and keep it real. Because they know so much about us, we tend to want to hold them close, lest we forget or lose track or feel alone. Cars, it seems, are no exception, especially if they are bequeathed.

I left my buggy with a full tank of gas. I doubt that often happens just as I doubt folks return rental cars filled with super unleaded. It felt dignified in the face of an otherwise utilitarian decision.

My consolation was that the dealer told me (while he was cooly cleaning the underside of his nails) that my car was going to be immediately auctioned off and shipped to a Caribbean island to live out its salad days.

"Really?" I perked up. "No more cold New England winters? No more road salt where the sun don't shine?"

"Nope."

"So I'm kinda sending it off to easy street to enjoy its golden years?"

"Yup."

"Like Moose chasing rabbits in Heaven?"

"Huh? Whatever, son."

So, Confused, give the old girl a final pat on the fender and thanks for a job well done. Then celebrate the relationship, tell yourself the car is retiring to the tropics (we all should be so lucky!!) and move on to the sweet sassafras smell of neeeeeeeewwwwwwwww carrrrrrrrrr! (And say it like you just won it on a game show!)

Hope this helped.

-Wally

Got a question for our advice columnist or trying to get rid of an excellent four-wheel drive used car for free? Contact him at cwn4@aol.com.

Ladies' Room

Dear Wally,

When we're out in public, my husband thinks nothing of going into the ladies' bathroom if the men's bathroom is occupied or simply too gross. This doesn't seem wrong to him in the least, but it does to me and I've said so. My question is: Under what circumstances is it ok for a guy to use the ladies' bathroom? It doesn't seem fair that guys should be allowed to come in and mess up the ladies' room. I know I sound old-fashioned.

-Pilar

Dear Pilar,

Your husband can hardly be faulted! Ladies' rooms are so much more civilized than men's rooms… I know this from recent experience and also from growing up with three sisters. The good news (for your gender) is that most red-blooded, he-men would prefer death or excruciating, cross-legged, throat clearing outside a locked men's room door to the humiliation of taking themselves three steps to the right and using the ladies' room. Not me! I'm with your husband on this and NOT going into an empty and perfectly good bathroom because of a sign with two extra letters (wo+men) seems like arbitrary folly to this full bladder. A toilet is a toilet is a toilet (except when it's a urinal). How's that for 1.5 gpf of philosophy?

I do want to stress that there are certain obligations that the male interloper has if he enters your gender's bathroom. If you have ever experienced a public men's room, then you know how vile it can be (and usually is). The defiling that grown men do when they think no one is going to scold them for being disgusting reminds us of the evolutionary angstrom (and I'm being generous here) separating us from the screeching, poo-flinging baboons in the monkey cage at the zoo. It is an axiomatic paradox that the more a guy's room is used, the less it *should* be used.

So gents, if you are planning on grabbing a skirt and jumping the gender fence on the rare occasion that the men's room line is longer, or that management has padlocked the bathroom at the Mobil Station because some budding Einstein mule-kicked the urinal off the wall in a drunken rage and caused a flood of Biblical proportions, or just because a backed-up toilet has volcanically erupted like a crap-packed Mt. Vesuvius and now it's too gross for anyone to clean except the Hazmat Spill Response team in full SCUBA gear, you will find a radically more pleasant, clean experience in the ladies' room. Hardly a secret. But if you enter, pride be damned, you must be a good ambassador for all other penis-wielders.

You must treat this sacred room with sisterly respect and dignity. Dig deep for it if you must. That includes lifting the lid and THEN LOWERING IT. You may think you can clear the seat with your torrent of well-aimed piss and subsequent game-ending dribble, but you can't take that chance. Not here. The stakes are too high. Save that business for the log pile or front lawn or between cars in the Walmart parking lot.

Proper ladies' room etiquette also requires fluffing up the potpourri with those ball scratchers of yours before you leave. It requires putting a triangular fold in the leading edge of the toilet paper roll as they do in fancy hotels. You might pluck some fresh flowers from around the dumpster and tactically strew them about. Create a lovely scene. You are visitor in a foreign country. If you are caught entering or exiting, you will bear the thorny crown of public ridicule and scorn. So the best defense is a good offense.

Invite your mocking heckler in to see what a good boy you've been. Make your momma proud (well, proud as she can be considering her son uses the ladies' room).

While I will avail myself of a clean women's room in a pinch (for a pinch?), when rolling solo, I will only do so if it doesn't mean displacing an already waiting woman. Operate under stealth conditions (read: no ladies in line) when no one but the heavy breather behind the Kwik-E-Mart counter is looking at the video feed from the security cam hidden behind the hand-soap dispenser. (How disappointing! A GUY!! Eeeek.) Always crack the door with your foot and send in a sing-songy "Helloooooooooo?" before fully entering or you might find yourself in perv's handcuffs should the room not be as empty as you thought.

Besides sating my biological urge to evacuate as expeditiously as possible in whatever bathroom is available, and at whatever cost to social order or decorum, when I travel with my five-year-old girl, I feel the veil of shame lift when I move toward the women's room door (even the handle feels pretty and clean!).

That is because we can all agree that sparing an innocent My Little Pony-loving daughter the wide-eyed, shocking experience of nine rounds with a men's room is a developmental imperative. We protect our young however we can. Momma bear? Try Poppa bear…

So, yes. Guys who behave themselves may use the ladies' loo. Just as ladies, if they dare, may use the men's loo. (And good luck with that! You could pee on the walls and it wouldn't make a difference.)

-Wally

Got a question for our advice columnist or have reason to believe he just might have been the person in the ladies' room immediately prior to you and just want to say "thanks"? Email him at cwn4@aol.com.

My Bionic Father

In the 1970s (so goes the premise for the hit TV series, *The Six Million Dollar Man*) the Government took a clinically dead, crashed Air Force test pilot whose steely on-screen name was Steve Austin, redirected six million dollars from a covert special-ops slush fund into his secret reconstruction (seven million dollars if you count the hair grooming/ blow drying—it was the '70s after all!) and created a part man, part machine, do-gooder superhero who found himself in compromising positions regularly (conveniently one-half hour every week, and always on Thursdays, to be precise. How fortunate for the network was that?!?) .

The Six Million Dollar Man, or the Bionic Man as we TV viewers used to casually call him, represented the then single highest line item in the Government's clandestine budget. An unimaginable sum. A sum so large that, like Austin Powers' conniving Dr. Evil, its mere uttering requires jamming a pinkie in the corner of one's mouth, twisting and chortling maniacally: Muwhahahahaha.

Six million dollars in those days bought you bionics, superhuman strength, immortality and invincibility in the form of new binocular eyes, titanium arm ligaments and armor-crushing hands run by computer chips and aircraft cable tendons. For six million they'd also throw in mechanical thighs that could catapult you 50 feet in the air like an electrocuted cheetah, should the exigency of saving the day call for it.

Plus being a six million dollar man back then got you in the sack with, and then got you married to (and then, sigh, got you divorced from) Farrah Fawcett Majors (R.I.P.). Worth every cent, at least in the '70s (and partway through the '80s).

It is nothing short of ironic to think that four decades later, after a massive military and healthcare industry build up, with the intent of ultimately keeping us more peaceful and healthier (which is cheaper than the alternative), these two budget hogs would still be first to the federal trough. Six million dollars today buys you less for your body, and yet paradoxically, it buys you more.

You can't swing a dead cat these days without hitting a bionic man or woman. Mechanical and fleshy prosthetics are readily available for every missing or malfunctioning part (including the unspeakable!). It's all good and no longer the stuff of TV fantasy. Organs, bones, teeth, fibers, synthetic hormones, all high tech, and all available and getting better, stronger and smaller by the day as the worlds of technology, military R&D, and healthcare converge.

My very own bionic father has a number of expensive and worthwhile technologies onboard, all co-operating with the original equipment. He loves to talk about it, which is the prerogative of old timers (guys, mostly) perched on diner stools sipping piping hot black coffee from thick, stained mugs.

Six million dollars, in today's dollars, spent thusly:

Eyes. Double cataract surgery. Laser-corrected vision, with new plastic lenses, means not only the end of brutally heavy, coke-bottle thick, gold-plated aviator glasses resting on the bridge of his nose after damn near 75 years, but the beginning of a new fashion trend in some developing nation. The chief of a small African village pries open the wooden slats of the "Eye Care, We Care" donation crate and 20 kids in need of glasses suddenly look like my dad because they are wearing the oversized glasses that have remained stubbornly immune to the whim of evolving fashion (unless we're talking East Germany circa 1957). These African kids will soon all have neck strain and look like retired bankers from Rhode Island. Except they won't.

A new heart. Or at least the mechanical components of one. The old one failed catastrophically three times in one day, eight years ago, and he's one of the lucky few to technically die three times in one day and live to tell about it. Additionally, there's a device with a computer chip in it that will kick-start

154

him with 200 joules of energy should the god-given automatic cardiac electrical pulse generator decide to go on strike. Ka THUMP (and hope you aren't driving behind him)!

Hearing aids. Oh the countless hearing aids! Each one like oleaginous snake oil peddling the irresistible dream of restorative hearing without the annoyance of actually having to put them in or absent the high pitched whine of the slightly less very expensive model purchased six months before with drastically inferior technology.

Teeth. After 70 years of faithful service and countless bon-bons and high octane coffee, the chompers are gradually self-selecting out of active duty and in their stead are placed composite implants, crowns and bridges, all working together like a public works project, to get the 4:30pm early bird dinner special choked down. As expensive as any public works bridge, too. And unlike a public works program, his bridge can be removed for easy cleaning while providing a source of boundless shock value for wide-eyed grandchildren or unsuspecting toll takers.

Hip. Titanium. Salsa lessons can now safely resume.

Also voraciously consuming the healthcare dollars on the way to the six- million-dollar mark are the battery of tests, pills, procedures and maneuvers associated with the above.

Six million dollars spent as well as I can imagine it ever being spent.

Call it $6.2 million for the bionic replacement finger that will be required when his giggling granddaughter finally pulls that index finger off. Pmphffffffffffffff. Wopwopwopwop.

-Wally

Got a letter for our puerile advice columnist, or just want to see what happens when you pull his finger? Email him at cwn4@aol.com.

WALLY'S PERSONAL PREFERENCES

Just Say Nayo

Dear Wally,

Do you like mayonnaise? My wife and I have lots of questions for you—some as philosophically deep as the Marianas Trench, others quite surface-bound, like this one about mayonnaise. You seem to be a little enigmatic, and a little opinionated at times if I may say (I'm a big fan of the column, by the way) so I'm figuring that all the *Dear Wally* readers might join me in wondering this about you? Or not.

-LB

Dear LB,

"Or not" is right!!

"Well we all have a face that we hide away forever, and we take it out and show ourselves when everyone has gone..." (from Billy Joel's *The Stranger*). Now why on earth would I tip my hand and expose the vulnerable, soft underbelly of my food predilections to a complete stranger? Or worse, quote Billy Joel? That be madness! But, ya know what? You took a real risk by heaving the question up on this public stage, so I'll go a round or two. And I'll try not to get too heady.

Here's my opinion in a deviled egg nutshell (eggshell?) gored by a toothpick and sprinkled with paprika and I'll thank you to keep this confession *entre nous*: I do not like mayonnaise (or bleached lard, or emulsified whale blubber, or adipose or whatever it is). I do not like it with green eggs and ham. I do not like it in a jar or can. I do not like it, Sam I am. I do not like it, and yet it is EVERYWHERE. Pervasive, sneaky, evil, oleaginous.

When I see mayo in my icebox (who really still calls it an icebox? What's my problem?) I toss it. It is sinfully wasteful to do this but I don't care. In fact, I relish (ouch) throwing this condiment out. I have no problem playing catch up (ouch) with my inner resolve and mustarding (ouch) the strength to escort it posthaste into the (any) welcoming dumpster. I don't even want the mayo jar in the recycle bin because no matter how well they melt the bottles down, the new soda bottles they make from them will still stinko de mayo, right? So the vessel goes right to the landfill, far as I'm concerned, to be smothered and capped by the relative redolence of spent diapers and maggotted fish heads.

I've had issues with this particular condiment (tuna fish lubricant?) since childhood. My mom (here we go, blaming the parents!!) used to spoon out milky, lemon-sized globules of the gelatinous goo from the wide-mouthed Hellman's jar (back when they still used glass) and splat it into an oversized, lime-green salad mixing bowl (it was the '70s after all). She'd then dump tuna fish from a can, toss in some minced celery, beat it senseless for a spell to the driving soundtrack of *Jesus Christ Superstar* and call it done. (This and my stretchy Danskin bellbottom slacks is all I remember about the '70s. Oh and the Dorothy Hamill haircut. I had both).

The resulting paste looked and smelled like cat food.

Meow.

It would then be smeared like viscous cake frosting onto a skinny slice of waiting white bread (that actually described me as a seven-year-old pretty well: a skinny slice of waiting, white bread) and sold to me (conceptually, anyway) as a delicious meal.

I was skeptical then and I'm skeptical now.

You can't fool the kids on the food front even if you wire the corners of your mouth up in a smile and dance a jig about how much fun (fill in the blank with whatever it is that isn't marshmallows) is to eat. Even good acting is bad acting and I've delivered some Academy performances.

Curiously, I'm greeted with puckered lips, a chorus of blecht blecht blechts and histrionic, pre-emptive guttural retches when even the most scrumptious thing is plated and presented to my four-year-old and she's decided that what I've cooked is really handsomely garnished rat poison on a platter. I'm no Emeril Lagasse, that's for sure, but I also haven't killed anyone with my cooking yet.

So all this isn't super good for my kitchen confidence. But for all the excellence and mediocrity in my day that I have proffered, and everything in between, I have yet to present her with anything containing mayonnaise. And ya also know what? I probably won't. I know it's a big food world out there, but I'm not giving her a passport to mayo land. Mostly cause it's too gross.

Knowing my long-term, fiery vituperation on the subject, my high school friends (bastards, in the loving sense) used to sneak industrial tubs of it on our overnight camping trips and dump it, five gallons (!?!) at a time, on my head whilst I slept.

I need a shower just thinking about it.

Is there enough therapy out there to fix me?

I fully realize this will result in a few cases worth of mayo being delivered to the *BlueStone Press'* offices, to my attention. I will smile politely and toss them like crap grenades into the dumpster.

So I guess the answer is no, LB. Not big on mayo.

-Wally

Got a question for our advice columnist or just want to join his Just-Say-Nayo support group? Email him at cwn4@aol.com.

Well, the unspeakable has happened: The floodgates of reader response have opened and the resulting deluge of heartfelt support for this strangely beloved condiment has hobbled the entire administrative *Dear Wally* staff. I had two assistants quit this week—one with lower back pains from hefting the bulging mail sack (and the other because I don't pay enough). So thank you.

Those of you who so actively dislike my dislike of mayonnaise have stood up and let yourselves be heard, and at some level I suppose I appreciate that. At some other level I wonder if these passions (and this unending free time you seem to have?) might not be better directed at, say, the anti-fracking movement ("frickin' fracking"?? Hmmmm. Cute AND fun to say, especially if mumbled! Could be bumper sticker material…) or protesting continental drift (North America and Europe ARE on a collision course at the rate of one inch per year and someone needs to start worrying). Or for those less politically active, sock darning?

Mayo.

As feared, some have even mailed me (care of the *BlueStone Press'* office) stolen (?) sample packets of the oleaginous crap to try and sway my stalwart, contrarian stance.

I won't be swayed by peer pressure or falsely framed "consensus." And no, I won't be your proselyte! At this point my repudiation is a matter of stubborn principle. And by the way, I don't live at the *BlueStone Press*, but if this economy tightens up any more, I might just.

I would like to share some of the letters, if for nothing else than to celebrate my impassioned, yet suspiciously anonymous, fellow Ulster Country tribesmen.

So here goes and keep 'em coming! (And next time, if you don't want me to goof on you, use a friend's name.)

Dear Wally,

Your derision of mayonnaise only confirms for us your place on the pedestal of inanity and insanity. Long live tuna salad!

Respectfully,

Mr. and Mrs. Anonymous

Anonymous,

Careful what you wish for. "Long living" tuna salad (especially unrefrigerated) will deliver unto you the kind of crippling, deep waist bends and diarrhea that will land you both in the Emergency Room, where you can be sure they won't serve you tuna salad. A family that sicks together sticks together…

-Wally

Dear Wally,

I must say that I was dismayed by your recent column regarding mayonnaise. I am an elderly woman living alone and memories of mayonnaise often keep me going. When I was very little I was left alone in my house by accident. My family returned several days later aghast at what they had done. Because of a large jar of mayo in the larder, I was able to fortify myself in their absence. Many years later while I was grocery shopping I dropped a jar of mayo on the floor (in those days only glass jars were used). The kind man who came to my aid ended up becoming my beloved husband!

Our five lovely children all grew up eating mayonnaise right from the jar, with big, greasy smiles that always warmed my heart.

So now, all I have are these wonderful memories and my jars of mayonnaise. You can't take them away from me, ever.

Sincerely,

Mrs. Edna Prince

Edna,

That's a beautiful story. If you remarry and your next husband also predeceases you, bear in mind that mayo makes a great embalming fluid. Keep him AND those memories alive forever!

-Wally

PS: Here's a dating tip—keep that mayo-shrine stuff under your lid for the first few dates, k?

Oh, and those glass jars are now collector's items. (You might be, too.)

Wally,

My mom says you shud (sic) not say mean stuff abowt (sic) mayo, I like it. I like it on a blt. Also with pretsuls (sic). Be nice to mayo.

-T (age 14)

T,

Tell you what—I'll be nice to mayo if you stay in school.

-Wally

Dear *BlueStone Press*,

On behalf of the Mayo Club of Ulster County, I would like to reprimand Wally for his incendiary and disparaging remarks regarding mayo. Where did you find this guy? With only 110 calories of fat per tablespoon, mayo is healthy, nutritious and delicious. Repent now and be saved. Join us as we bring this amazing condiment into the spotlight it deserves. Visit us at www.mayohealsall.com. Look forward to hearing from you.

-Jonathan

Jonathan,

Jonathan, my man... Your letter had grease stains on it. You really love mayo so much that you can't write a two-sentence proselytizing letter urging me to repent without getting mayo schizzz on it? What's your problem? If this is what salvation looks like, I'll take Hell. At least the mayo will be in a liquefied state.

-Wally

Recipe for Wally,

Yummy Mayo Dip

Mix:
1C mayonnaise
1C Parmesan cheese
1 C chopped artichoke hearts
1-2 cloves garlic

Then:
1) salt and pepper to taste
2) bake at 350 degrees for 25-30 minutes
3) enjoy

Reader,

I was ok with the recipe until the last step. I rewrote it for you.

1) salt and pepper to taste
2) bake at 350 degrees for 25-30 minutes
3) flush

-Wally

Well, I'm out of space. I'm glad I could be a lightning rod for the mayo faithful. If I write a piece on how much I hate $20 bills, will you all send those to me as well? Let's try! Please send your letters of concerns (and your Andrew Jacksons) to me at cwn4@aol.com.

A Salute to Neil Armstrong

Astronaut Neil Armstrong was a national treasure and a real-life hero. I can't think of any heroes today who we can look up to without first having to pay nine dollars. (Even if you want to see the super-hot Rachel Weiss and super-cool Daniel Craig (James Bond) work out in Stone Ridge, there's still a daily gym fee.)

"Captain America" Armstrong was our square-jawed agent in a proxy war with the Soviet Union to see who could tag the moon first. Back in the '60s, we all knew the moon was made of cheese, but we needed to make sure it was AMERICAN cheese (and, specifically, liquid orange Kraft cheese from the nozzle of a can). So we actually created a spaceship that paid homage to that cylindrical Kraft whipped cream/spray cheese canister. (The Chinese were working on a spaceship that looked like a beef and broccoli take-out container and ran into some aeronautical drag co-efficiency snags, but it did have a cute little wire handle.)

We shoved Neil Armstrong, Buzz Aldrin and [the other guy] up in its nozzle, filled it with unthinkable amounts of explosives, called it Apollo 11, and lit the flippin' fuse.

Who signs up for that gig?

Ummm, hey... can you hold on to this ticking bomb while we shoot you into orbit? You might blow up, in fact the guys before you did. There's no air up there (and no heat) so you have to wear this fishbowl on your head. By the way, you could float away into nothingness at any moment or get bonked by space debris going faster than anything we can even measure. Also, we have never done this moon landing thing before, and we don't know if you will be incinerated when you return, or if you will even get to return. There are 100,000 knobs and dials in your spaceship. Don't touch the wrong one at the wrong time or you are toast. So is your expensive (and only) ride home. There's an instruction manual under the seat in case we lose contact. Be careful with it, it's the only one.

There's a week's worth of food, and then, if you are not back, you guys will have to eat each other. (For the ease of the history books eat [the other guy] first.) You will have to pee in your spacesuit. There's one small window, so learn to share. Also, there are no doctors, so don't get sick. And even if there were doctors, there's no one alive who knows how to fix stuff in a zero-gravity environment.

If even ONE of you farts... (Three guys in an airtight spaceship for one week? Dream on...) it's with you the entire time, cause that one window? It doesn't open. So just think about it.

And unlike James Bond, you won't get a stunt double.

But if you survive the trip, and you don't get abducted or anally probed by Martians, and you don't crash into the earth or drown or get eaten by sharks in the Indian Ocean upon splashdown or bring back some celestial pathogen that wipes out mankind, we'll put your faces on the Wheaties box and later, when you are old, let one of you go on the Howard Stern show and get verbally abused with questions not about your lunar experience but on your current Viagra usage.

Oh, and you had better not be scared of heights cause this is pretty much the top of the game in terms of that. (If you have ever seen launching pad footage of the astronauts walking into Apollo 11 while it is still bolted to the ground, you'll agree it's nauseatingly high. And that's without them lifting off even a single foot.)

Who the hell signs up for that? Some sinewy manifestation of courage—the original get-r-done guy.

Neil Armstrong left his boot mark on the moon's ass for the sullen, pickled Soviet chimpanzee in low orbit to screech at each time it passed. So we won that war, I guess.

Now that the silly jingoistic chest-pounding is over, we humans from all countries get to enjoy the major haul of science, technology and jobs that happened as a result of superpower space exploration. And projects such as the International Space Station (which is currently rusting, but anyway…) have been fantastic at uniting the human spirit and heart regardless of geo-terrestrial-politics.

Think of it! We got pens that write upside down because of NASA. We got Velcro. We got *Star Wars*. We got Space Invaders. We got Moonpies and RC Cola. We got little toy rocket engines that my cousin and I could ignite and shoot at each other from behind trees until he got hit in the nuts and I got grounded.

As a people, we got orange-flavored Tang (approved by moms AND NASA!). We got a branding logo for MTV. McDonald's even got an opportunity to project (with lasers) their golden arches on the moon. What a great billboard, right? Now that he's gone, Neil Armstrong would certainly haunt that advertising executive from the grave if I had to look up with my honey on a romantic night and see the Mickie D logo etched into the moon. (Talk about being made of cheese…!)

None of this could have happened without Mr. America and Buzz Aldrin (whom Neil was gonna shove out the rocket door and feed to the monsters on the moon if they showed up hungry, he later confessed). And let's not forget [the other guy] (whose name I forget) who drew the short straw and had to stay behind. (Bad luck, Cinderello. You get to scrub the orbiter's floors).

Neil, thank you for your courage (and for letting Howard Stern goof on you in later years). But you know what? Don't drink that sugary crap, Tang—stuff'll kill ya. Know what I mean?

-Wally

PS: The other guy? Number three? Michael Collins.

Letter to Cat

Dear Wally,

Are you a cat person or a dog person?

-Laurel

Dear Laurel,

You guess. Here's a letter I once wrote to our enormous black cat, Teaser.

Cat,

I don't like you rubbing up against my leg. I never have and I never will. We go through this every day. This is not new material. You should be chasing mice, not fishing for compliments by parading your oversized, puckering exhaust pipe back and forth at us and our guests every living moment of every living day. Put that tail down! It's almost like you are giving my steel-tipped work boot a huge, pulsing neon bulls-eye.

I trip on you because you are constantly underfoot. Constantly. I hear cats are very perceptive. And barn cats wily. So what is your problem?? The more I recoil, the more persistent you are. Plus you leave cat hair everywhere. That is the primary reason you are an OUTSIDE cat. (That, and I find you pushy.) (And the word "barn" is right there in your title.) I put the word "outside" in capitals as a courtesy in case your eyesight is going. (I have reason to believe it is indeed going because there are STILL mice around and it looks like they are having a holiday on your watch. Are they? Are you on the take or something? What are they paying you to leave them alone and pester me? Whatever it is, I'll double it.)

Cat,

How can anything lose as much hair as you and not be completely bald? I think you grow it just to leave a trail of it everywhere you go in case you get lost. Yet you never stray far from the front door. I bet you say, "If I can't be inside, at least my hair can." There's a path of snarly black cat hair from the front steps of the house to the hood of my car. There are muddy cat paw prints (don't try to blame it on a raccoon, I've got your number) on the hood of my car that crisscross left and right, up and down. Are you practicing *salsa y merengue* on my car or something? Shouldn't you be CHASING MICE? You fight the other cats when we put breakfast food down so I know you have the fight in you. Why don't you turn that hostility toward a good cause? (Ummm, like getting field mice!?) Would it kill you to think about your work a bit more instead of bickering with your fellow barn cats? The only catfight I want to see is between Britney Spears, Lindsay Lohan, and Miley Cyrus and it involves Jell-O. (Are you listening God?)

Cat,

I know you hate my dogs and want to see them garroted. Unfortunately, the feeling with them is mutual. There's a reason for the expression "fighting like cats and dogs." (There's also a reason for the expression "raining like cats and dogs," but I have no idea what it is.) I'm sorry, but we fell on the dog side of the cat/dog lover's fence long before we met you. Don't take it personally. We're too old to change. The inside is for the dogs, the outside is for the cats. I know winter is coming and you think you will be cold. You won't. Trust me. Try to keep some of that hair on your body. It will help. We even made you an insulated cathouse. (It's in the barn. Do you remember where that is?? If you get lost, follow the mice.) Why do you refuse to stay in it? Are you upset there is no room service? Instead you park your keester smack-dab on the stoop of our front door, where each morning I trip.

Cat,

I know you have self-esteem and co-dependency issues to work out. Never mind the abandonment issues you have with your father. But, I assure you, strutting like a three-dollar whore on my front porch is not the answer. It is pathetic and I hope you can get the professional help you need.

Remember this final thought. I'd like you two hundred times more if you pulled your own weight around here. (And if you didn't leap up and pull the heads off of birds in mid-flight.) And I'm sorry I inadvertently ran you over last year with my car. I felt horrible. I'm glad you are feeling better. I feel like we've gotten a little closer as a result of that incident. Not much, but a little bit. Under my car is not a great place to nap, you know…

Cat,

My appreciation of you is fickle and foxy like the wind and, at times, downright questionable.

-Wally

Got a letter for our advice columnist? Or are you a crazy old cat lady who wants to letter-bomb him? Here's his email address: cwn4@aol.com.

PS: Simmer down, Cat Lady, this is a bit of a goof. Teaser is pretty cool, actually.

Tomato in Winter

Come here you little tomato. Let me see you up close. I question your authenticity. It is, after all, mid-winter and the only thing that grows around here these days is frozen mud. We are in our New York deep freeze and you, (how can I say this respectfully?) *you* do not occur naturally. August? Yes. February? No way. Yet, I still hoist you up at ShopRite and consider you. You are not cheap, either. Maybe I will and maybe I won't. My little daughter needs veggies, even if you are a fruit posing as a vegetable. Or a vegetable posing as a fruit. You are the Senator Joe Lieberman of fruits and, yet, the Senator Joe Lieberman of veggies! A garden politician without a party. Kissing babies, pressing the flesh, and looking trustworthy from afar.

You are an easier sell than broccoli to my child, and a three-point lay-up next to a plate of Brussels sprouts that will work for me (if broiled, mind you) but will not work, in a cool million years, for her no matter how much butter (or even chocolate sauce) I drizzle on. It begs the grander rhetorical question, to wit: How many root veggies must I eat before my organs shut down and walk off the jobsite? I'm sweet potatoed out, God d'yam it! Is anyone out there listening?????

You, tomato, will do in a pinch. I want to spell you with an "e" at the end, even though I know it is wrong. Tomatoe. There, I've said it, like so many people first write it before cocking their eyebrows and realizing something is queer about the spelling.

I want summer back, I guess, and you are a proxy agent for my wishes, though it is a foregone conclusion that you (and your mealy texture and cardboard taste) will gravely disappoint my palette. Still…

You are shipped in from California or somewhere where you are picked prematurely by people who get to wear shorts and work on their tans. Grrrr. You fit the minimum requirements for ShopRite Corporate, for sure, as you ripen your genetically-modified self in the back of a cold, dark, semi-truck and haul through the slushy likes of Kansas at 3am. Hammer down. Mud flaps flappin'.

You are doing the best you can, so I don't fault you for trying and I don't mean this grouse to be personal. It's more of a systemic indictment.

Vermilion in exterior hue. Translucent, waxy-white on the inside. As if you've been frozen and thawed a few too many times (not unlike my tenth grade geometry teacher). Your odd size (speaking of geometry) is that of a midsized mountain goat's inflamed testicle. Something is off. Wish I could harness a more pleasant image, but traumatically inflamed billy-goat balls come to mind.

You are displayed on a visually alluring and angled bed at the supermarket where you are surrounded by other red orbs. We see you accented by the jacked up, contrasting verdancy of basil, itself an equally suspect imposter this time of year, as we customers stamp stubborn snow off our boots. If there was such a thing as veggie porn, a tomato and basil display right as we walk in the store would be it. Especially if there was mozzarella packed in chipped ice on the edges. Who wouldn't cobble together a nice summer salad, even if "summer" belongs to those half a world away?

But what choice is there?

Catsup? That doesn't really count.

I will eat you anyway and will put on my best, pasty, New England winter puss.

-Wally

Got a question for our advice columnist or some tomatoes you are now no longer interested in eating?? Email him at cwn4@aol.com.

Makin' Hay...

Part 1

Blood pulses out between the knuckles on my left hand to the beat of *Macarena*. I've got no Latin blood in me, but apparently I have Latin arterial rhythm. The cut has happened not because of the sharp edge of the pocket knife I ritually carry when baling hay, but instead, it comes from the dull edge of a blunt 9/16th box wrench that has failed its grip under much force. It's a hag of a cut, torn as it is. Pain forks around looking for a willing path back to the neural Muthaship. There are plenty.

I can feel the tetanus (and all other dust-borne agents of infection) celebrating this opportune gift and dancing a holy jig across this suddenly permeable border crossing. I rip the white tee shirt off my back and ball it up. But for the lack of pretty girls in blue jean cut-offs, and an iced down cooler, and, well, me bleeding, this is starting to look like a Mountain Dew commercial—the sepia tones and slow motion of a half-naked, farm-strong guy leaning over well-worn equipment on a blisteringly hot day. It is sometimes a wispy fine line between the smile and the wince.

I'm squatting beside a broken hay baler from a different era. It is attached to the International Harvester "M" tractor of my youth. The combo idles on a steep undulation of freshly mowed garbage grass that hasn't been plowed under and reseeded since the Dutch dairy farmers who lived here for 100 years threw up their hands and moved on. And that was a generation or two ago. The whole tractor/baler set up is a tad precarious. I'm trusting brakes that were made when FDR was first elected President.

I've got hay down and horses that expect to be fed this winter.

We're in the grassy crotch of two mountain ranges here in the Hudson Valley. I can see both monsters from anywhere I stand on my farm's 150 acres. Between them and under my feet is a wide sea of viscous clay in which nothing grows. It is capped with a veneer of topsoil that allows for this vegetative toupee. This sloped meadow is no place for a narrow front-ended, and thus very unstable, tractor, even if the brakes hold.

I know this tractor like I know a childhood friend. Somewhere in my belly, I can feel the literal tipping point when I drive these hairy hills. I stay just shy of it somehow. There's probably some formula to calculate when she'll upset and crush my rib cage, but the seat of my pants and a primordial sense of self-preservation have proven effective thus far. Straight up, straight down. Them's the rules.

To the west, the storied Catskills loom. The ghosts of resort-packing Jewish comedians from the '60s and '70s rattle and chortle. Though it could be more of a lonely wail. Stale shticks and affordable air transportation to other places successfully threatened to turn the so-called Borsch belt into a cinched up economic castration device.

It worked.

Moss and rot nip at some of the once mighty, now mothballed resorts. The erstwhile pride of the Catskills is these days a raw reminder of how unforgiving time and opportunity can be. A few formerly pristine golf courses are now tangles of thicket bushy with neglect and arrogant crabgrass.

Some resorts have survived but they gimp in the shadow of their former majesty. The entire region now has its collective thumb hooked out for a ride on the gambling bus which a certain number of voters claim promises an uninterrupted trip to Job-ville in the great state of Prosperity. A certain other number swear it's a flume ride straight to Hell by way of logarithmic social decay with the sound of jangling slots being our deserved death knell.

Gambling may or may not come to the great state of New York. Passions run hot on this issue. There are certain laws of physics that also apply to politics, inertia being one. So we wait it out and see what happens. Whether it's legal or not, everyone up here is already gambling on something.

I'm inclined to put $20 on red. Except I spent my last $20 on fuel for the tractor.

The other way, the formidable spine of the Gunk's ridge stabs the sky. This is a top rock-climbing destination in North America. Glimpse west from the New York State Thruway near New Paltz and the sheer rock wall looks like the square jaw of a pissed-off Marine. Shawangunk conglomerate is a coarse-grained sandstone deposited 400 million years ago. It defines the region topographically and when we are not scraping the adhesive, red-clay goo from our shoes, we are standing on some form of this rock. It's also about the hardest stuff in the world. I had a well driller curse my name and walk off the job when he hit the conglomerate bedrock on my property that caused him to bust three multi-thousand dollar bits. As if it were my fault...

I've buggered a lot of stuff up in my day, and I can own a lot of my problems, but advancing and retreating ice sheets from thousands of years ago and the stubborn nature of bonding carbon molecules are beyond even my doing. The irony of a hard headed guy having to contend with hard headed material is not lost on me. It seems poetically just in some sense.

Here I am, genuflecting in a hay field. At the altar of, and tending to, a broken baler with a profusely bleeding paw. I'm also giving the darkening sky the royal stink eye and I'm hiking my shorts back up a notch on the off chance that the mole-searching, red tailed hawk who makes himself present whenever I cut the fields might have a better go of it without seeing my butt crack.

I am working these fields as a single dad of a 5-year-old girl 90 miles from my last home which had skyscrapers and pickpockets.

My now disposable tee shirt/rag has its work cut out for it. I wrap it around my hand in a tight knot to keep pressure on the hemorrhage. I go once around with a swath of duct tape borrowed from the baler's twine holder. It's a worthwhile trade. I'm a volunteer EMT here in the country and know that this, while ugly, is neither life threatening nor more important than the hay. This show must go on, even if I have to elevate the extremity, which is step two for controlling the bleed (step three being a tourniquet and subsequent loss of limb in a worst case scenario). Alone in the field, arm raised high above my head, I give the appearance of an earnest schoolboy with a question. As if I'm asking the universe if I can excuse myself from this lesson and take a piss.

You, in the front row!

High above, the gun-barrel gray cumuli are swirling like mottled cotton ball turds in a toilet, chasing the cerulean blue skies asunder and reminding me that my already tiny, midget window for getting this hay baled, off the field and safely into the barn, is closing. For any hay farmer, the obstacles to task completion are myriad and each conspires with the other to thwart. Pressure from inclement weather is the tooth-barred, rangy, lead dog.

Got to get the hay up.

Part 2

Knock down the alfalfa, clover and timothy (as we say in the hay-making biz) and the clock starts. While others don't keep track of consecutive days of rain, or fall asleep slumped over the short band weather radio with the reek of the morning's bacon still in their hair, we hay farmers are acutely aware of imminent and past moisture trends. We also have a skeptical ear for anything coming from the slippery lips of the pros. Get burned a few times by inaccurate forecasts and the clowns on the evening news start to look like clowns on the evening

176

news. If we've learned anything, it's that we've learned nothing.

Get burned a few times by inaccurate forecasts of love, and, well, now the weather feels predictable.

Once cut, rain immediately switches from essential to apocalyptic as relates to the grass. You ride that emotional orientation like it's a saddle made of barbed wire. You need three full days of pleasant weather, fully operational equipment, and old fashioned human strength to not lose your shirt making hay. And by pleasant weather, I mean the kind they copy from an archipelago and Photoshop onto brochures. Plus when you are gunning for the other side of the hay field with old equipment and looming clouds, you'd better have some duct tape handy. You will need it.

Making hay sounds so damn pastoral, like you are in an ascot and loose fitting clothes guiding a facile process that nature is all too capable of doing herself. The train of truth has left that station with sparks flying from grinding steel wheels. Haying is kinetic, temperamental, exhausting, frustrating, and yet somehow, strangely satisfying. You will go to bed, or rather fall into it, at the end of the day fully spent and barely affected by the tinnitus of loud tractor that will accompany you through the night.

If you are too tired to bathe, you will take a second, scratchy skin of chaff, dirt and dried blood into those sheets and all but ruin them. Your spouse, if you have one, will likely not be happy about it.

You will be too tired to soothe the raw abrasions that bale after relentless bale have caused your skin. You might have a sympathetic partner willing to apply a soothing nard, but this is unlikely if you are between the bookends of very new or very old love. This space is ill-defined, and demands butt up against expectations which butt up against needs. You will go to bed with raw abrasions and wake up into the healing process.

177

You will be hard pressed to find anyone willing to sign up for a helping of this hay-making experience, at least all phases of it.

Maybe except for the few remaining who have done it as kids and who want a quick spin down memory lane. They will gimp away when the conditions sour and the rewards seem unattainable. That might be as quick as an hour. And you will close those eyes for the last time that day with a smile, in your sullied sheets, despite all the discomfort and maybe even in spite of the loneliness of it. That is, if you got all the hay in before the rain. Loneliness isn't exactly the right word. More like the solitary Zen of it.

The triad of "what, when and how" upon which every task rests, is mostly beyond control. Pretty much the only variable we control is the "what," and one out of three is fairly crappy odds. Try driving a tricycle with only one wheel. Try flying an airplane with one wing. Try fixing a baler with one hand.

I do a quick calculation: Broken baler, wounded hand, gathering storm clouds. All three legs of the variable stool have been compromised. I feel waxing anxiety in my core. It's an uneasy boil—the kind of greasy unease that anyone about to get dumped knows in their viscera. Half of my Chi has been nailed to the floorboard.

Out on the freshly shorn meadow, the long French braid of adequately dried hay waiting to be baled no longer looks like a three-acre long cruller made of dollar signs. It looks like rotting hay I'll have to pick up in two weeks by hand and throw out because the fickle baler will not take it in.

In this case, not only will I not win, I will actually lose large. There's a difference. Simply not winning is soft. Clean. Not winning and actually losing is jagged. Avulsive (which isn't a word, but should be one). I peek under the shirt to see how my body is healing itself. I'm a good clotter, I'll say that much. Someday, I'll add that to my inchoate and irreverent business card which currently boasts such hirable skills as war waging, cliff diving, ostrich racing, pimple squeezing, baler fixing and swashbuckling. My hand is a shit show but I'll not bleed out this day. And the world needs more swashbuckling, to say nothing of baler fixing.

There is not a soul in any of the cars whipping by on nearby State Route 209 that cares a wit for my troubles. They are off to Walmart and Ellenville. Or Kingston. Got to get something. Got to do something. Got to be somewhere. I know, I'm in this stream often. And I'm not looking for sympathy. It's worth mentioning this. Everyone's in their own head and that's the cost of doing business as a human, sentient being.

I just want a little more time before the deluge forces us all to twist on our windshield wipers and grimace through the sheeting. I will have neither windshield wipers nor an actual windshield. So of course, no rain at all is the best plan. But tell that to the clouds…

The old farm machinery gods, being what they are, have determined that more human sacrifice is in order, and my wrench slips on the baler's busted flywheel bolt accordingly. They must be appeased and it's rarely the pretty or innocent they go for. Usually, it's the nasty grizzled types who toss themselves on the rusty John Deere tine. Many hay farmers are already missing digits or parts of digits. (Rare is the farmer who wears a wedding ring for this very reason.) Plenty walk with a dipping gimp or bowed out leg owing to some man versus machine mishap that is all but guaranteed as a function of time. When squared off against machines, we may be smarter but we are far less durable.

My tough hands are no match for steel. The tough hands of the farmers around here tell a probable story of accidents, defiance and hard work. There is consistency in farmers' hands that transcends all geo-political orientation. A brotherhood and sisterhood of tool grippers, we are. Just a couple chromosomes and millennia ahead of our vine-gripping simian brethren, is all. With hands upon her hips, my grandmother used to say to me on the family farm she ran, "Well, you might just get going. That shovel doesn't dig by itself." Or equally annoying, "That barn won't paint itself!" In other words, calloused hands (good) don't make themselves.

Calloused hands are *de rigueur* this many miles from an office, and possibly even a cracked, bleeding badge of honor amongst a certain set. That we might measure a man's contribution or worth by the amount of unsloughed flesh still stuck on his nard-worthy hands is an interesting notion. Pink, fleshy man-hands, conservative or liberal, are a quick route to judgment in the blue-collared world. They all but say, "You are doughy and soft. You are a laggard who hasn't paid his dues, and I'm carrying you out here in the dirt, where it matters. And I am unduly burdened."

I'm amused thinking about the task the high-end Asian callous-eating micro fish would have were any of these farmer types to dip their grease darkened mitts into the spa tank otherwise reserved for the feet of rich women. (This will never happen for farmers unless those tanks are filled with diesel and there's a tractor axle part soaking in it to clean, but it is amusing to consider.) Would the Cambodian spa fish choke on the load of a farmer's calluses and float to the surface belly up?

Spending time thinking about divorce and Cambodian spa fish is time I'm not spending on getting my hay up before the rain.

Got to get the hay up.

Part 3

Old farm equipment will break when you need it most. It will break when your hay is down and when there's rain in the forecast. Old farm equipment will kick you in the teeth and then go ahead and kick you in the crotch for good measure.

A hay baler will break when NAPA Auto Parts is closed or FedEx is three days out with the part you need from a rusting donor machine in a farm equipment graveyard in central Ohio

(Ohio, the still-throbbing left ventricle of farming). It's not just me being a curmudgeon. This is axiomatic. I hurt in the teeth from this truth.

The more hay that you cut, the higher the investment. The higher the investment (economic and emotional), the greater chance there is that something you need to not break, actually will. And then the harder it will hurt. Such is the nature of an investment.

How we jigger up a Plan B in the face of Plan A failure is the measure of success in the field, whether or not you are actually in a field.

Here in the actual field though. I have a few tools with me when I bale hay that are universal in the service of Plan A, B, C or even Plan D. I stuff my pockets with them and they serve me well. To wit: pliers, a hammer, an adjustable wrench, a 9/16th box-end wrench and a pocket knife. The right tool for the job, or some permeation of this, is the basis of a hackneyed, but plumb and level, cliché. I cheat it to an extent with my stripped down, generalist tool kit. Most problems are beyond the scope of the tools at hand but not beyond the scope of tools generally available. Who wants the weight of superfluous tools? No one whose pants are already falling down. Which would be me.

So we do the best with what we have. We weld scraps of angle iron. Torch, grind, drill, secure with baling twine, fasten with our ever-present duct tape. Got to get those shredded hands and clicking brains around a solution when the weather window's closing, the hay is down and the horses are hungry. But you learn to be resourceful because there is no other option. You divine resourcefulness like a dowsing water witch because resourcefulness is the mother of necessity. And we love our mothers...

Those once experienced and twice burnt pay homage to the notion of preventative maintenance. Things in their care are greased and oiled and checked pre-emptively, versus reactively. Do it reactively and you will pay thrice. This law knows no limitations and you can easily muster a support group of farmers, politicians, parents, or divorcees all ready to sit in a circle in some church basement, heads in their hands, sip coffee and tell the overlord of this truth their first name.

By all accounts I'm a gentleman farmer, which is more a reflection of the scale of my operation than of my disposition. The gentleman part of the description seems questionable when I drop the F-bomb at the slipped wrench and bury it to shank depth in the field's dirt with a fling as my grease-rag of a shirt stains dark red with deoxygenated blood from my shredded hand. It's more like an F-machine gun than an F-bomb. Screaming "F%#k" "F%#k" "F%#k" "F%#k" repeatedly feels cathartic; it is pure and punctual. And with a paucity of other relief options, it is the next best thing to not being hurt in the first place (see aforementioned desk job).

Six hundred bales is a good haul for me and this stands in direct contrast to the operations of close farming neighbors who scale up with new equipment, flat fields and bulk fuel storage, and who can gammon me with 10 times the yield. Those big picturesque round bales that dot the landscape and look like straw Ring Dings? They are damp inside. They don't need the same number of drying days as the square bales. Cows can digest slightly fermenting hay. Horses can't. So it's back to small square bales and the fickle, antiquated, temperamental machines that (sometimes) work well enough to require only a few tools.

It hardly seems worth the enormous effort to hay the minor league's infield, except there is something far more valuable than just the efficient loop of providing for the horses from the very land on which they stand, stamp out flies and defecate all day and night.

The process (cutting, tedding, raking, baling, picking up and storing) is symphonic and inexorable. I've been doing it on and off for 43 years and it's grounding. Sometimes with a crew, sometimes solo. It is my past and my recalibration. For those with particular goggles on, there is metaphor and meaning in everything. This is my blessing and my curse. I hunger for imagery and connectivity. A narrative thread to suture the human experience. It helps me make sense of life. Even if the thread is biodegradable Brazilian baling twine.

I was once told that you only need two points to draw a straight line. The first point is easy. We are all given the first point. It's the second point or the third, fourth and fifth that prove elusive. Locating them all in the same axis is rare.

Connecting the points? Cutting hay, tending to it, picking it up as a metaphor? Continually fixing an essentially unfixable baler? Or one that will fail me at a critical moment? I just look at the projects whose lives and mine have intertwined. Coincidence and/or destiny. Euclidian and/or philosophical.

I've unwittingly invited these complicated projects and obstacles into my life. Or they find me. Like taking a few steps back, getting a running start, and smashing headlong into a one-ton, round bale. And doing it repeatedly. It might budge, but it also might not.

There are things depending on my ability to connect the dots. Horses for one. Me for another.

There's also a little daughter in my life who is depending on stability. She wants, and she deserves, at least two of the points to be in the same plane. Those points cannot, for now, be her parents. I've got pliers, a hammer and an adjustable wrench on me, but they are undersized for this job. I already have one bad cut on my hand.

I think those with the sort of predisposition to seek meaning in life in every little thing ultimately find themselves wearing out the hair on their knees praying, staggering out of bars or perhaps gam deep in hay fields with bandaged extremities. Still, there is something to everything that happens. That's the macro.

The micro, however, is what needs my attention right now. There is no way out of this predicament save for sheer obstinacy and a dash of silver-haired MacGyver. There is no cavalry riding over the Gunk's pugnacious crest with a new inflated tire, or twine knotters that actually work.

If I get this all together, I will pick up hay by myself with one and a half hands. What's THAT there mean?? Ha!

Back in the day, my high school friends who were beefy from football would swagger over to help pick up hay on my grandmother's farm. They would be laid to waste half an hour into a six-hour, 2,000-bale hay pick up. If I was an EMT back then, I'd have administered oxygen.

Juan, the eternally 35-year-old Basque farm manager with a green card and cheap cigar breath, scrappy as a one-eyed bantam and lean as a ligament, would ride my friends relentlessly for their failure. He would stamp out Muriel blunts on, and dance on the grave of, America's imminent mediocrity, as reflected by its doubled over youth in the face of real work. "Is this the best you got?" he'd scoff.

The notion that everything is better elsewhere is precisely the revisionist history that so many treat themselves to. This person is better than that. That person is better than this. This situation is better than that. That situation is better than this. The grass in Spain may have been greener then, but the grass I am baling here and now is as green as it gets. Now, to just actually get it baled...

Part 4

I need a bolt from the hardware store for my broken New Holland 273 hay baler. It's a long trip—longer than the five actual miles it is. Soon it will be raining and I labor under this pressure. I'll drive my patiently waiting, beater pick-up truck whose reliability is best described as iffy. My old-timer friend

Harley's lifetime allegiance is with Chevy. And Coors Light. I have a Dodge. "Bad choice," he snorts, every time he sees me. He ribs me that the reason Dodge makes pick-up trucks at all is so that the driver can throw a bicycle in the back and always have it handy for when the truck breaks down on the side of the road. Apparently Chevys never break. And Budweiser is pee water. I'm nowhere near being ready to be enlisted as a foot soldier in a proxy war between chest-thumping corporate silverbacks.

At any given time it feels like half of the things I own to get work done might either not start or not stop.

I make this distinction between work machines and big boy toys because I have very few "toys" as such and plenty of work machines—and there's really no overlap in this thrifty Yankee's estimation. I don't have an ATV or snowmobile or fishing boat or flat screen TV. I have an Adirondack chair that I don't use. It sits next to a second Adirondack chair that isn't used either. Neither now, nor before, when I was married, and it occurs to me that Adirondack chairs mostly represent the patient promise of relaxation, which is sometimes good enough. I've found that the people who buy them are the people who need them are the people who don't use them. Same for hammocks.

I do have a tractor, old hay equipment and a truck. And to be fair, I have a palliative hot tub which I have justified to help mitigate the deep body aches of the farm work that often hobbles me.

My pick-up truck is now a work machine but it was once, and recently so, a big boy toy. It was owned by a 19-year-old, Ohio-based kid named Sean who jacked it up and made it super loud. He worked at Burger King. He poured his humble and hard-earned fortune into this amplified mechanical love affair and finally walked when the sheer economics of keeping a continually breaking toy on the road snuffed his enthusiasm from the wallet inward. At some point, his blind infatuation with this truck pulled into a gritty focus and the relationship was no longer viable. His first divorce. Even the pros will tell you: relationships require work, but then again you shouldn't have to work toooooo hard…

Enter me. A willing buyer for the stamped-steel challis of his curdled dreams. I have my own dreams and they are fresh. This truck was, and is, a series of important lessons on the dirt path to a man's maturity, be he 19 or 46.

It is primer black (I could care less). The AC has long since given up the ghost. The cloth interior has been impregnated with the indelible pungency of cigarette smoke and meatball-wedge farts—both from a source other than me, as I quickly tell new passengers.

The electric windows work only when the buttons are stabbed with proper conviction. The truck is strong enough to pull a tree over in low gear. The four-wheel drive works, which is my insurance for a snow plow guy who doesn't show up for work because of this or that. It also is stick shift, which is my insurance for a starter or battery that doesn't show up for work because of this or that.

In some twisted way, I look forward to the day I get to pop the clutch to start it. That day will arrive. When it does, and I roll my 5,000 pound truck down the driveway in neutral and pop the clutch, and that engine purrs, and I will not need to prostrate myself to the scheduling whim and humiliation of AAA dependency, I will shriek loudly. Possibly as loudly and as victoriously as Howard Dean did in his career-ending, Presidential bleat.

Blaaaaaaaahhhhhhhhhhhhh!!!!!!!!!!

This truck will take me from my hay field to the hardware store for a one-dollar part that will allow me to get back to the hay fields before the rain comes.

This truck has enormous, oversized tires that serve no obvious function other than to elevate it above the next bull calf's jacked-up truck and thus trumpet jungle-law dominance.

This display of superfluous lift feels positively primal. As if the calculation was crystal clear to young Sean that the higher the truck, the more attractive he would be to a potential female mate, and that its brutish bigness and mighty stature would immediately rocket said female into estrus, make her rip her clothes off and sate a 2,000-year-old procreative imperative. In short, a bad-ass, monster truck means the 19-year-old will get laid.

My five-year-old daughter has named the truck "Lilly." What a shameful moniker compared to Bucephalus or whatever it used to be fancied. Alexander the Not-So-Great might name his steed Lilly.

Lilly gets horrific gas mileage. I will spend ten dollars in gas getting a one-dollar bolt. With more advance planning, I would have a few spare baler parts on hand. But unless one plans to reconstitute a hardware store on their property, guessing what will break on an old baler is a losing proposition. It's like playing Whack-A-Mole with nuts and bolts.

I do feel powerful driving my truck and though I'm not out to pick up chicks with it, I can sort of channel the Conquistador mojo of its former owner, Sean, and see how he might equate this monstrosity with something powerful and possibly beyond his ability to articulate. This truck is a strutting peacock with chrome plumage, a lift kit and lights on top to illuminate God knows what.

And now, in the back of this erstwhile chick-magnet is a boner-killing car seat.

As with my tractor, I need to hold on tight because it bounces a lot. I get knocked around leaving the field and getting to the driveway, which is its own special rodeo owing to the fact that driveways are expensive to maintain. I argue to the unconvinced that it's cheaper to replace the entire suspension and transmission than it is to truck in gravel.

Soon I will be one of those people stomping the accelerator, hoping to not get T-boned by distracted people on their way to somewhere important via State Route 209 as I pull into the flow of traffic. Soon I will be one of those people I notice from my tractor seat.

I pass a farmer out in his field kicking up a plume of dust as he tills the soil before the clouds burst and his soil turns to unworkable, wet clay. This day, his equipment works. This day mine does not. That's how the life wave breaks out here.

One-dollar bolt? Check. Hardware store? Check. Rain clouds? Check.

Part 5

The cacophonous din of Lilly the truck's "performance" exhaust system is almost unbearable as I pass through the old Dodge's five gears and her engine screams in either agony or ecstasy. Hard to tell which, and anyway, sometimes it's a fine line. "Performance" as it relates to this loud exhaust system is code for broken, loud and obnoxious—actually a bragging point of this thing's former 19-year-old owner. One man's ex is another man's treasure... I'm a few decibels south of getting a ticket for noise pollution.

There is nothing performance, however, as it relates to the loosey goosey steering system. It's almost aerobic exercise keeping this 5,000 pound truck on the pavement. This relationship takes a lot of work.

The 2000 Dodge was just designed that way and I'm reminded of a laughable line that was peddled to my dad when he bought a brand new Jeep Wagoneer in the '80s, and immediately brought it back to the dealer because it pulled really hard to the right. The chain-smoking, oleaginous salesman looked him right dead in the eyes and told him Chrysler/Jeep had designed that safety feature into the car so that if he as a driver happened to fall asleep at the wheel, he would gently and harmlessly drift onto the shoulder versus into the oncoming traffic thus minimizing the potential damage and saving the lives of innocent children. The engineers, you see, did this for us sleepy, irresponsible driving fools.

It's hard to wonder why my old timer friend and Chevy aficionado Harley doesn't give me more of a hard time for buying Dodge than he already does, but I'm convinced that since the '80s, and their post- Chapter 11 bitch slap/reality check, they've rescinded that insulting, hubristic "safety" line of sh%t on a shingle.

I've used the term "all over the road" as it relates to others' behavior that doesn't make sense to me, or that pendulums through plumb rational on the way to extreme irrational. But in the strict sense, still technically between the yellow and white lines that are rightfully mine on this errand as I drive a barely cooperative truck, I am that guy.

Closing the driver's side window on this sweltering day offers little acoustic relief as I head to the hardware store to get the one-dollar bolt that will fix my baler and hopefully save the cut hay from the imminent thunderstorm. But it does offer some quiet, so I put the window up. It just causes me to sweat more and pour my own body stench into the melting pot of other smells that the unslakable seat cloth cheerily absorbs.

So when I, dressed in only stained, cut-off shorts and an International Harvester baseball cap, see a discarded fur coat on the side of the road, on this hot day, it seems surreal. Who still has these politically incorrect things? Who litters with one? I fully expect to see a hamburger wrapper discarded by some inconsiderate litter-pig, but a fur coat??

Turns out the fur coat belongs to the adult male coyote who owned it up until the moment he was struck by a car. The animal is splayed on the roadside like a science experiment and

189

probably a day or so into death. I'm no taxidermist and I don't watch CSI, so the timing is really just a guess. But I didn't notice it yesterday and I would have. A dead coyote holds the same fascination for folks as does a car wreck. I slow a bit to get a better look.

It lies on a bed of improbable wind-whipped vegetation, crushed beer cans and jettisoned, man-made detritus.

We instinctually know that coyotes live in the area. We hear them. We see the evidence they leave behind. They are close. They thrust and parry with the human boundaries and lurk in the voids between the worlds. They have wolf-like mystique and instill a disproportionate scale of fear in us, though they are essentially just wild dogs with no direct interest in humans. We see dogs all the time and they don't cause us to slow our cars and ogle. Unless they are dead and formerly wild and the mystery of their viscera is smeared on the hot blacktop.

My daughter is saucer-eyed at the mere mention of coyotes, though she's never laid eyes on one, dead or alive. Coyotes are large-toothed props in the imaginative narrative that plays in her young head—some hirsute, wolfy distillate made from *Little Red Riding Hood* thigh meat and our farm's yapping lapdogs' slobber. The coyote is found licking its chops at the intersection of innocence and evil. She's convinced she'll be a coyote's lunch someday.

This one danced the line too closely. Its carcass is hard proof that we are closer to the wild than we may care to admit. And maybe closer to the immutable laws that govern nature and physics than we may care to admit, for these laws are neither reliably kind, nor warm, nor particularly fuzzy. These acute laws can easily leave you splayed and with tire tracks on your back.

I slow down, as does everyone, to get a good look at the dead coyote.

My, what big eyes you have!

190

Had.

The speed with which nature reclaims its own is remarkable. Already the carcass is starting to flatten, decomposing from the inside out. The maggots are busy, busy, busy. Vibrating with industriousness. In just days with this heat it will be flat as the discarded coat I thought it to be. And then with some rain, and tenderized by the tires of a few distracted, texting drivers, it will be pulverized into nothingness.

It all happens so quick. Everything. And this from the guy who gets misty eyes in the supermarket's diaper aisle when his daughter shoots overnight from Huggies size two to size three, or steps on the bus for Kindergarten. *Tempus* friggin' *fugit*.

Coyotes travel in packs but are only really hit by cars in the singular. Or they travel in a pack that then abandons their dead, leaving me with the roadside impression that they move through life and death rather alone. Heretofore, my lifetime dead coyote siting count is five. This unlucky fellow makes six.

Raccoons, on the other hand, are often creamed by cars in pairs with a sorry splat of juicy, mottled gray/blue entrails connecting the bodies. They mate for life. There is something wistful and yet sublime about the dual raccoon road kill. Their quest for something better on the other side? Their commitment to the journey? Their earnest attempts toward that end? Their dying devotion to each other playing out on asphalt like a Shakespearean tragedy?

When I see the dual road kill, which feels frequent up here in the country, I think of the loving grandparents who have been married for 50 years despite the overwhelming odds. She wipes his chin as he watches TV and grumbles about the President. He brushes her hair because she can no longer lift her arm. They have survived the drift. And when one dies, the other doesn't live more than a week.

My lifetime dead raccoon count is three memorable pairs.

I shut the truck down in the parking lot and my ears are ringing. I pass the piles of discounted bark mulch and resplendent plastic Adirondack chairs that decorate the hardware store's front with the elusive promise to others of manicured landscapes and relaxation. I will not be trading in the currency of that rainbow-hued dream today.

I pull my bloody shirt over my head because going in bloody and shirtless seems the greater of social gaffs. With my duct-tape bandaged hand, and tarred and feathered by the day's complications, as I've been, in machine grease, blood and hay chaff, I am a sight to behold. I doubt I'd let me in if I were Tony the owner.

I walk to the back where the bolt display, a veritable cornucopia of parts, takes up the back wall. It is an unlimited salad bar of steel fixin's.

The dream I am purchasing for one dollar is that I will be back in business with my working New Holland baler, picking up hay just in time to pirouette and give the rain cloud my raised and bandaged, irreverent middle finger.

Ahead of me in the checkout line and purchasing light bulbs and dish soap is a sweet elderly couple hunched over matching canes. Sweet, except that they are yelling loudly at each other about who forgot the money and bickering about the required wattage. He looks to be a nanosecond away from bonking her on the head with his cane and her eyes are filled with a lifetime of sloshing brown vitriol.

Raccoons. Traveling by twos. And my lifetime count suddenly goes up to four.

Part 6

The tiny sheer bolt I need for the incapacitated baler serves the purpose of breaking when the overall machine is exposed to excessive stress. It's sacrificial in this respect. If I inadvertently

192

bale wet hay, or pick up a hidden stick, the mysterious plunging, packing and knot-tying gizmos that make this old baler turn windrows of hay into stackable bales, get buggered up from the resistance.

As is so often said, something's gotta give. By breaking, this one-dollar bolt saves more intricate and expensive parts from getting destroyed. There is so much potential and kinetic energy in this hay baler's relentless, flywheel-driven, packing-hammer that, yes, in crisis, something has to give. But for the carefully engineered timing set at the factory, the baler would destroy itself in seconds.

I wish relationships had sheer bolts. Maybe they do and I just didn't go to the right hardware store.

Driving home with my hardware store part, I notice that the dead coyote lies at the base of the "Welcome to Kerhonkson" sign. The sign is new. Well, newish. It's half of a nice touch. Unlike other signs, in southern towns, the opposing side of this sign doesn't thank me for being in Kerhonkson as I leave. No "Y'all come back, hear?" No, "You are now leaving Kerhonkson. See ya next time!"

It's one of those things that is just obviated by the next town's welcome sign and thus stabbingly New Yorkerish, which is to say, right the hell to the point.

I've taken to calling my upstate town Rainhonkson—a snarky, but well-earned, bastardized contraction of "rain" and its proper Dutch name, Kerhonkson, which I've loosely translated into "son of a friggin' loud-ass, honking goose."

We are in the historic, tight-channeled, migratory path of Canada geese. They honk way up there in the cumulonimbi, complaining forcefully, I'm convinced, because it's always either raining or about to rain. This might just be the melodramatic, gravel kicking of one (me) who has been soaked in a hay field by rain a few too many times. That bellyaching aside, when it is nice out, my zip code is about the most beautiful place in the world and I will not deny Kerhonkson this distinction.

Kerhonkson's other claim to fame is that just before the British burning of Kingston in October of 1777, all important documents were secretly moved here for two weeks before finally being relocated to Albany. They were temporarily housed next to what would eventually be the strawberry ice cream in the freezer chest at Stewart's, just below the rainbow sparkles and to the left of the *Playboy* magazines. Kerhonkson—the original Revolutionary transfer station. We did our part.

A look around and it's still anchored by rolling farm lands. Different faces and equipment, but the game is still the same. So are a lot of the families. Generations later, the same steel-belted work ethic permeates: Work the soil, reap what you sow.

Recently, farmers have banded together to fortify the fledgling interest in larger scale, locally grown produce. There is strength in numbers. There is also safety. There's also a general awakening to the economic prudence of locally spent dollars. To our collective credit, we have started to move the needle as we scowl at the bald inefficiencies of trucking produce cross-country and munching out-of-season indulgences. Some local purchases make sense when you look at them in a different light. Locally grown carrots? Sure. Locally grown toilet paper? Not so much.

We have farmers' markets and roadside produce stands in this area between Kingston and Ellenville, which in EMT parlance, presents the area with an economically shockable cardiac rhythm. In some parts of upstate New York it's not even worth taking the defibrillator out of the bag.

Willing customers, some full-timers, some weekenders, find the experience of pinching produce shoulder to shoulder with neighbors compelling and authentic and charming enough that they are spending some money here and less at the malls that bookend the 30-mile Route 209 corridor.

So economically ravaged has this area become in the last few decades with the shuttering of businesses that I counted the protesters to Walmart, which is coming to Ellenville (just south of Kerhonkson) on one hand and still had enough fingers to pick my nose. Which I did.

In Kerhonkson proper, the economic kernel of which is a four-way intersection comprised of two gas stations, cigarettes, beer, gas and lottery tickets constitute the bulk of the gross domestic product of this small town as it gasps for air.

Besides a single bar and a single funeral parlor, which are uncomely neighbors of each other to my thinking, we have a single laundromat, a beer barn/liquor store/market, a bank, a pizza parlor, a flower shop, a pool-and-spa supply shop, an auto body shop and a post office.

We also have a lawn equipment place and a Chinese restaurant, which unlike in other small town commercial contractions, are not one in the same establishment here. We have a new pop-up, high-end, coffee shop open but a scant six hours a week, and those six hours are on Sundays. The owners are taking the town's temperature as it relates to this sort of higher end enterprise.

I'm reminded of what a history professor once told me: Most settlers died from arrows in their backs, not from arrows in their fronts.

We had two diners but one burned down and smelted itself on the years of built-up, flammable grease. Its charred remains are scattered on the chalk-lined asphalt of its own parking lot. It looks like the debris field of a plane crash, albeit a plane made of wood, vinyl siding and a couple deep fryers.

It has flattened like a decomposing coyote.

An empty and waiting roll-off container stands by patiently. Because of the purported asbestos, various governmental agencies have shined up their boots and shown up to take control. Except no control has actually been taken. The authorities have been squabbling over what to do and have succeeded pretty much only in prohibiting the mess from being touched whatsoever, by anyone. For over a year, erosive rain water has carried the alleged toxic material between their spread legs and folded arms to tributaries and rivers that a different enforcement division of the same agency is trying to protect.

In waste removal, as in politics, as in Kafka, inertia and silliness are at play. I feel like a monkey sitting on a jungle vine eating a banana and watching two other bickering monkeys relentlessly slap each other with the bananas they might just as well be eating.

The remediation plan that no one will pay for is a wildly expensive asbestos-tenting contraption. We could buy a new ambulance with that money. We could acquire the next town over for that money. While we stand around hangdog and frustrated that we can't just shove all the crap into the dumpster and move on, the irony is that any good Samaritan in a black Ninja suit caught cleaning it up in the middle of the night will be arrested.

There is an Arlo Guthrie song to be written here.

Nearby, a sign warns of a $350 town fine for dumping and it makes me smirk every time I drive past.

Some frustrated resident tacked up a sign that reads "10 months and counting." That was four months ago. Another jokester clamored over the rubble (in the middle of the night, I presume) and righted a two-top table, set two burnt place settings, arranged two opposing chairs and placed a rose between them as a center piece. It looks classy, in a charred sorta way.

Our greased diner is now a greased political pig that hogs far more newspaper ink in its death than it ever did in its life. Budding politicians have roped it into their platforms with promises of progress and tidiness—perhaps leveraging a handy metaphor.

Oh, and another thing about Kerhonkson—

According to the US census, for every 100 women, there are 100.2 men in this town of 1,600. Hey now!

I want to sneak up in the middle of the night and spray paint that factoid on the town's sanguine welcome sign.

I rub my eyes as I drive by in my oversized, loud-ass farm truck because I swear the sign says, "Welcome to Kerhonkson. Now get back to work, fix that baler and get that hay up before it rains. And while you are at it, fix that exhaust pipe."

Part 7

I never really know how I do it, just that I do. There's something vocational and something intuitive about the process. There's also a little hocus-pocus going on. I have no formal training in fixing broken farm machinery—just a degree in English Literature from a fancy school which is utterly useless out here in the dust bowls of Broken Balerville. That is, unless I need a cream-colored parchment rag with Latin calligraphy on it to check the tractor's oil. James Joyce mixes with machinery grease the way rain water does.

Never have I met, in flesh or steel, a more entitled diva than the late '60s square hay baler. When there is hay down in the field and rain on the way, when the stakes are the highest, she's the belle of the ball—the one whose fancy must be tickled, whose superstitions must be indulged. She is also the one to whose ears the crushed eggshells under my raw feet are deafening. I tiptoe through her untethered moods and ride the floppy sin curve of her manic inclinations. She's to be coddled.

197

She's defiantly into her mid 40s, tempered by her convictions and flatly dismissive. She's no longer young, and yet not quite old. She has erosive rust but maintains her structural integrity. She's on unpredictable terrain and she is weary—the way an old thigh may or may not successfully lower an old body into an old armchair. You just never know. And the whole scene is cringe-worthy.

When I first got her, I loved her. I was anesthetized with awe. She was used by hard hands and then discarded. But I didn't care. She was showroom new to me.

Now, when she decides to stop working, it will be for whatever reason, or no Goddamn reason whatsoever. This is the prerogative of the self-anointed and the unjustly entitled. Those for whom life has slid their way on a greased chute. These types? Their sense of order is insular, their actions self-serving. I labor under this capriciousness. There's logic somewhere under that stratum of hay chaff and grease, but it's lost on this farm boy and anyway, it seems like daisy-bending whimsy. Some sort of test of my mettle or of the stalwartness of my course.

You don't dare tell her that her wheels are square.

The repair I need to make requires that the heavy flywheel at the end of the baler's PTO shaft be spun backward until the holes line up. Then I can put in the new sheer bolt and be on my way. Running the machine in reverse is as uncomfortable as watching a cat throw up. Partially digested hay comes back out from the packing chamber in convulsions. The machine groans and creaks. Its soul is confused.

I take my pinkie finger and a piece of twisted wire hanger and try to jab the decapitated segment of sheer bolt out, but it's not budging. I drop the F-bomb just because. I've clamped the replacement bolt between my lips because I need my hands free. It dangles like a chilled, smokeless, chrome e-cigarillo.

There's very little room to work and I'm doing so with a bloody, bandaged hand that still hurts plenty. Using the back of my hammer as a fulcrum in this tight space, and the blade of a long screwdriver, and a pinch of MacGyver, I'm able to push with the force required to pop this stubborn piece out of place. Evicted, it falls to the grass, lost instantly to a cliché of needles and haystacks and to it I say good effing riddance.

Except for the red tail hawk that is busy picking off the luckless snakes and field mice I've thrashed or clobbered with my machines, there's no one around to share my enthusiasm, to celebrate this small victory. But this is one of life's sweet moments. It's a triumph of intellect and troubleshooting. It's a triumph of calmness and perseverance. It's even a triumph over mechanical inertia, for if I didn't successfully take corrective action, this machine would never work again. As in never, ever. No one else would care enough to be bothered.

My success shouldn't be built up to more than it is, big picture, but it should be acknowledged. And for a temporal instant, until reason gets the better of me, I'd take it over a winning lottery ticket. Such joy from such simplicity on the tail of such complexity. There are plenty of other ways this could have turned out, and none of them nearly as sublime.

The ghost of Juan, a good man, the industrious, resourceful, Basque farm hand who showed me as a kid how to fix stuff while keeping his boot on the throat of American accomplishment, is in a Spanish bodega somewhere, taking a deep drag on a cheap, full-sized cigar that was likely rolled between the thighs of Cuban virgins.

If the New Holland 273 baler could talk, she'd address me thusly: "Ok little boy. I've made you suffer enough for one day. You may now continue with whatever it is that is so, uhhhhhh, important to you. Just be more careful next time. I'm special and need to be treated this way. Adore me and fear me and exalt me and respect me. This is what you *do* in a relationship. I'm in charge and you do not control me. Just remember that. I will break at any time of my choosing. And while you are at it, you can get me a snot-green bottle of Perrier with no ice. It's not mistakes you are making, though a genius you are not. Your errors are volitional and the portals of discovery. That is all. Get back to work."

Part 8

A lesson I keep learning over and over is this: Check the easy stuff first. The problem is, I never really learn this lesson. I tell myself I do, but I don't. And it's frustrating because it's the calm, measured me that understands this idea. *After*. The panicky, OMG me is usually first to the accident scene and assumes incident command. Millions of gears, chains, parts, blood, gore. It's a universe of variables, each competing for prominence and attention. Usually, the culprit is the obvious choice but it takes an elusive clarity and calmness to identify it. Therein lies the rub. Adrenalin bombs and calming nards are mutually exclusive. And we know which one always shows up first to bully.

With respect to the broken baler I'm trying to fix, the one that keeps me from the task of baling downed hay, filling the barn and feeding the horses this winter, there is no repair schematic, no decipherable manual. You see, it's easy to panic when you are doing 60 and about to run out of pavement. It's not much different than freezing when taking a standardized test because you have come across a question that cold clocks you and makes you forget everything but your name.

The way that life nudges me toward help is that I'm forced into a thought-provoking, blisteringly hot, death march up the long driveway to the garage to get the right tools most every time the baler breaks. So 10 minutes and a change of environment may be all it takes to calm right down and think. To gain perspective by broadening the lens.

My nightmarishly long driveway has been historically eroded by the very cloud bursts that now threaten to ruin my hay. It feels lunar in terms of its quirky topography. If it were a treadmill at the gym, my gravel driveway would be on the steepest grade setting and the motor would be smoking. The actual drive-surface gravel on my driveway has slid off the compacted road base like molten cheese from a tipped slice of pizza. I've run marathons and been less exhausted than I am when walking up it on a humid summer day.

Bored and curious horses amble over to the rustic oak fence line that runs parallel. They come to check me out. Unless they are being ridden, they eat all day long, and that's it. Nothing else to do except maybe keep an eye on a theoretical predator. There are none in these parts but instinct is a powerful thing, and their easy life here notwithstanding, that instinct isn't breeding out anytime soon.

They come to check me out. I rub Honey's nose and tease her that she's getting a fat ass. She's a rescue from an abusive situation. Horrific the way some people treat animals. Angelic the way others treat them. She has turned into one of the better lesson horses for young kids here on the farm. Her second chance is some kids' second chance, too. She was literally snatched from the horse-meat auction guy. Honey caught a lucky break from a good woman, and her appreciation for an unthreatened remainder of her life on rolling green fields and in my custody is palpable. She is joined in a snort by Art, a 16-hand, nosey pain in the butt who likes breaking my fences and farting shamelessly. If there's such a thing as a newspaper tabloid on the farm, Art is the chief editor and sole reporter. He's always up in everyone's business. I imagine them nickering to themselves—oh, just Wally again. Baler must have broken again.

They each rub their necks on the one-by-six red oak boards that I had custom cut at Waruch lumber mill 10 years ago. It's as if they are shaving off ticks, or scratching a deep itch. The sun-silvered boards have at this point lived out their useful life.

They bow under the strain of scratchy horse necks. Frank at the mill promised a decade out of the boards when they were first cut and stacked so neatly in my truck. He was dead on.

They are now rotting in spots, mostly around the nail holes and rusty screw scuppers. I have tied a few failing boards up with baling twine—as stop-gap a measure as they come. Farm ghetto through one lens. Budget through another. Lazy through yet a third. As the boards have shrunk, torque and split, tormented by the Hudson Valley weather extremes, and smoothed by the hair and oils in the horses' skin, they have developed what some call rustic character and what others a foot away might consider a run-down look.

The cedar posts I previously hand-cut and buried to hold the boards are also decomposing away from the center where they meet the moist soil, in a way that resembles neglected teeth rotting to the core and in dire need of root canal.

The amount of work that went into this project makes me shudder, even a decade later. Cutting, drilling, digging, pounding, dragging. Time's mighty hand knocking my efforts down one frost cycle at a time. I remember thinking I'd get a lifetime out of this fence, despite what I inherently knew to be true. Guilty, I suppose, of wishful thinking. It started out so shiny and strong. Even that fresh-cut smell felt invincible. Failure seemed so improbable at the time and that's the gloss of optimism. If I replaced the entire fence tomorrow, I'd be the same sucker who thinks it will last forever.

I can't replace it now because Waruch Lumber has gone out of business after 30 years and Frank, who could tell what state a log came from based on the growth-ring pattern, has had to seek a new job in a different industry.

What I have is what I have, and I'll have to get creative if Art busts the rail with his big neck.

This trudge up the driveway is the equivalent of giving myself a middle aged time-out so as to not say something or do

202

something I might quickly regret. Or go down the wong wabbit hole. I dish time-outs out to my recalcitrant daughter on the rare occasion she's rude or if she just needs some time to think about her unacceptable behavior. My actions happen when contrition is nowhere to be found. The space is sacred somehow. The required silence is viscous and her hollow scowl of shame and disapproval usually heavy. There are different parental schools of thought with respect to the judicious use of time-outs, but they have worked for me, regardless of which end I'm on. This self-imposed one is working for me, as usual. I start thinking about broader options.

Good EMTs approach an emergency scene with a wide lens and open mind. Better ones do this while the adrenalin is pumping. The best can do all of the above while applying pressure to a spurting femoral artery. Tunnel vision can have deleterious effects for the victim, be they made of human flesh or agricultural machinery's steel.

It's got to be the same for mechanics and family doctors. And times 100 for airplane mechanics and cardiac surgeons.

The anxiety of unreliability out here in the field under the gathering rain clouds takes a righteous place in my squirmy innards. I have a wrench and a replacement bolt and with them, I've fixed, or will fix, a problem. There should be no more discussion. I have made a repair and I'm now ready to scramble to the task's completion.

I should be happy, yet I feel tarred and bruised by time's hasty passage. I hate being such a victim of vagary and whim, just as I loathe perceiving myself a victim of some inanimate object's, or animate person's, actions. Especially when there's an imposing deadline, like rain. It's not a kind place to be. Stupid baler, breaking all the time. Don't I treat you well? Take care of you? Give you my blood? What more do you want from me? Is this not a relationship you value enough to salvage? If you'd only talk to me once in a while…

There is no help line for this baling machine's many woes when they come at my face with no warning. I've got no recourse within the trouble-shooting chapters of torn, oil-stained operator's manuals, which strange folks collect and sell online, (maybe not so strange juxtaposed to the truly strange folks who sell diseased toenails online). Rarely are real problems as easily solved as they are in the manuals, if you are lucky enough to have them in the first place.

Anyway, the art of fixing a baler is lost on all but a few marginalized old timers sitting around the fire's dying embers on wooded stumps in the nippy winter of their lives.

I'll be one of those bastards someday as I acquire a familiarity with a contraption that travels in the fast lane to extinction. But not today. Today, I dance with the rain clouds and charm a fickle iron dame into compliance with a one-dollar sheer bolt martini and a bloody hand to show for it. It's a sweet little victory.

This aging diva baler-chick and I have a date that's back on to get this hay up before the rain comes. We'll get it right, this relationship. We're just coming at it with different needs and expectations. We are connected by a one-dollar sheet bolt, which is the first thing to check when trouble shooting and the last thing that is actually checked. We need each other. At least that's what I keep telling myself.

Part 9

This New Holland baler's 12-inch, spring-loaded tines kick up dust and scratch up rows of hay into her five-foot-wide maw with the frenetic determination of 100 Ethiopian chickens.

Different tines then flick the hay into a flywheel-powered packing chamber driven by the tractor's spinning PTO shaft in pounding, chain-driven, iambic pentameter. Get unlucky enough to have some ill-fitting clothing buggered up in the works, or give this hungry machine any opportunity to snag you by wearing a watch or wedding ring, and you will be baled into a 40-pound, twine-tied package without remorse.

Baling wet hay is also a bad idea. The metabolic break down and fermentation process involving tightly bound, damp hay can result in one of life's biggest counter-intuitions: Wet hay catching on fire. If you didn't know better, you'd never see it coming.

Plenty of corner-cutting farmers trying to beat the rain have leaned into this truth the hard way as weeks later, their hay barns turn into county-wide marshmallow roasts. Choosing not to be one of them means choosing to be affected by the weather—not good for my inner control freak.

On this day, with rain on the horizon, hay on the ground, and my hand bandaged with duct tape, something else is amiss. Flywheel's been fixed with a one-dollar sheer bolt, yes. But...

The baler sits off level and I notice it the way that only a parent notices the slightest fog in their child's eye. Something, not sure what, but something is wrong. My Ah-Ha moment comes as I dismount the tractor and do a walk around.

The baler's far tire walked itself off the rim just enough to go flat and bind up in a drive chain. No time to find a new tire. No way to fix the old one, though I'm tempted to make a tire out of duct tape. (Has this ever been done? Somebody must have!) Thirty more seconds of operation and I'd have a broken drive chain and sprocket that would shut me down for days.

Absent other viable options, I hack off the already ruined tire with a battery operated Sawz-All and gun that puppy to the job's completion on its cold, steel rim. (Note: driving on a rim only is as ghetto as it comes—a huge no-no in the world of machinery. The wince-worthy task is marginally less wince-worthy when doing so on grass versus the town road. But still...)

Somewhere in a small Basque Spanish café 3,000 miles away, as he ponders semi-forced retirement, and as I drive a lopsided baler on its clanking, tireless rim under gathering storm clouds, my mentor, Juan, is shaking his head and throwing the remaining gulp of warm red wine down his gullet. My embarrassing "get it done" fix has his greasy, guilty fingerprints all over it.

I'm partially superstitious when it comes to making hay. I try not to look at the black barn cat perpetually licking his nuts as I drive down the driveway with the tractor and baler combo. Because my baler breaks at will, and for little or no cause, the swamp of confidence has been drained down to the gooey muck.

So, with no faith, superstition is all I have left to work with, short of buying a new baler. Through trial and error, I've encountered slightly fewer baler breakdowns with the following shenanigans: tractor throttle exactly three notches below the max RPM. Second gear only, no matter how confident I'm feeling. My old Keens and my lucky shorts. I also keep a five-dollar bill in my right pocket. This seems ridiculous even to me, but it falls squarely in the category of "Why the hell not?"

There's time to consider things on a tractor seat when the machinery actually IS working. There's a combustive drone that can open up contemplative space between the ears. One is then beyond the reach of chirping cell phones and thus isolated from that temptation of communicating with other human beings. And one can receive this as a gift of introspection or one can take it as an extruded span of sanctioned torture that sullies the pallet with the heavy aftertaste of spent diesel and aspirated dust particulates.

I try not to get too lost in my thoughts because, well, it's dangerous. A fellow died last year when the PTO shaft of his brush hog broke loose and crushed his skull in. He may have been daydreaming, or not, but either way the Sherriff's K-9 unit found him a few days later in the weeds with his tongue sticking out. One eye open, one eye closed.

Off the childhood farm and into college, I was beset with a sense of nostalgia I now attribute to my mother who, though departed in physical form, was then always acutely aware of the fleeting nature of time, of its slippery evanescence, in a way I sense is exclusively reserved for the mature of soul.

How silly, I thought 35 years ago from this very same unpadded tractor seat, watching her watch me bale hay as a teenager and spit out hay from my mouth as a man-in-training, how silly to see her literally so happy to be connected to this process, and to the earth, and to her children that it brought tears to her eyes. It takes something like the opposite of youth to realize the meaning of happy tears. The sweet reek of fresh-cut hay is the signature of eternity—an instant, generational portal to simple summer nights on my old farm. When I was the kid. Not the adult.

Grandma's voice rings in my head—"That hay doesn't pick itself up!" Juan's voice rings in my head. "Get the F back to work." The grazing horses that will benefit from this hay through winter's dark, strangling fingers have their rumps to me. The July fireflies are spinning up their illumination reactors and primping for their tepid evening flits. My daughter is safe and content with her mother for the first of the three days of the week they share. My hand has finally stopped bleeding, which also means it's started healing.

All around me I see bales. Glorious, hard-earned, *dry*, bales. They look like scratchy, 40-pound, five-dollar excretions from the baler that has finally stopped being obstreperous and started being cooperative. I am grateful for the break. I will now press Lilly the Loud Truck into service once again as I load her up with as many of these things as I dare. I will crank her radio and blast country music as I hurl hay bales with puncturing contempt at the chalky clouds far above my head. I will involuntarily wet-dog shimmy out the dust and chaff from my eyes as these bales then fall back down to the truck's bed in a lazy heap. Take that, stupid rain cloud! Figured it out before you did…

Part 10

I printed and laminated the following note and then left it on my roadside, self-serve farm stand on August 15th, after an entire summer of being ripped off. The laminated note itself AND all the hay were both stolen within THREE days!

Hay Thief,

Here's what's uncool:

ME busting my hump cutting, baling and picking up hay in the blistering heat, putting it on the stand here for six dollars per bale and YOU paying three dollars per bale. Or you only paying the 73 cents that's banging around your floor. OR YOU JUST NOT PAYING AT ALL.

This charming farm stand is self-serve and is based on the honor system. HONOR. LET'S DISCUSS. Is there something about you paying only what you want, versus what I charge, that is honorable? Would you do this at a gas station?

Right. Didn't think so…

You back up your car with the best intentions maybe. Hungry rabbits, weedy garden. Whatever. Then the fact that no one is actually watching you is just too tempting. You can't resist short-changing me because you know you won't get caught. Muwahahaha.

Maybe you rationalize paying less by saying, "Oh, this hay isn't that good." Maybe you feel globally wronged by other vendors and by not paying me, it is a cosmic payback to all the crappy vendors you feel are out to get you? Maybe you feel noble in your actions? A warrior for socio-economic justice?

Well, consider this, old Greasy Hands McGillicuddy: Old machinery breaks down all the time. It costs me money and time to buy it and fix it. Fuel. Sun screen. Gatorade. Duct tape. Vaseline (don't ask).

Making hay is also dangerous. Ticks, snakes and bees are just a few of the natural risks. Spinning PTO shafts can break and seriously injure or kill me or anyone nearby. Maybe you think 40-pound square bales appear out of thin air?? Like the clouds just poop them out? You are not at a cocktail party here and these bales are not *hors d'oeuvres* for you to Hoover up.

Turns out I like making hay. But I'm not in the business of GIVING IT TO YOU. I have bills to pay, like taxes and food for my family. My resources get stretched when you fail to complete the financial transaction. I'm saving for my kid's college and you are screwing her. If she ends up changing light bulbs in Grand Central Station, I'll hold you responsible. So screw you.

If you are short the money one day and your rabbits or garden are going to die, fine. Take a bale. Make it up next time you drive by. I'm not unreasonable. Things happen. But this is getting back to basic manners and you, Hay Thief, are getting a failing grade.

If after this warning you continue to steal, under the nose of the police barracks right behind you, and your god who has either failed you in your value system or who is feathering a nest for you in cheater's Hell, which I hope is at least as hot as my hay fields on a July day, then I'm not sure what...

Actually, yes. I DO know what. If you continue to thumb your nose at my hard work and the law of Western Society as it relates to buying and selling, then I hope that a nice, juicy deer tick jumps off the bale you have stolen and chomps you in the nuts. (Not sure why but I'm assuming you are male.)

Stealing my hay—that's what's uncool…

See you in Hell!

For all the rest of you excellent, honest customers, have a sunny, pleasant day!

-The Management

Afterword

Wally Gets the Last Word

Dear Wally,

It was me who took your hay, and your handy plastic-covered note too. I use it to chop meth on when I need a little pick-me-up. You write a lot about your own feelings, but I don't think you've considered mine. That hay is for my children to sleep in. It's a full time job fighting the SAFE act for the NRA and attending pro-fracking rallies in Albany for Exxon. It takes a lot of money to put gas in the truck, and have any leftover for a can of Full Throttle and some Twizzlers for the kids, with the high cost of bullets and all. People don't pay as much for firewood as they used to either. And don't tell me about your tree-vails with a broken bailer—try keeping a Home Depot Huskie saw running for ten minutes without some part falling off, you'll see. THAT's what you might call the dark night of the soul. If you want to fight about it, you can find me at Cumberland Farms, playing scratch off and hoping like hell that they get Nevele open so I can play for high stakes and get out of this rental trailer. When I strike it rich, I'll even let you swim in my fish pond at my Sovereign State of Jedidiah, just over the hill. Just don't bring any of your tax-and-spend liberal friends from Massachusetts or Rosendale. It's guvmint regulation and people who charge for hay that's destroying this country.

-A Citizen for Responsible Fracking

PS: I'd appreciate it if you put out some eggs out at that stand of yours too. Seems like everyone else is raising chickens, why not you?

Dear Citizen for Responsible Fracking,

Thank you for your string of gently intended non-sequitors. I'm feeling the love.

I'm not looking to scrap with you in a Cumberland Farm parking lot (eeeek, can we at least make it Stewart's?), though the thought of rolling around on asphalt drenched with the leaking lubricant from your gas guzzling truck's oil pan IS appealing. Sort of like Jell-O wrestling. Except not.

What would be accomplished by you chasing me in and around the parked cars and throwing crystal meth at me (does that hurt??)? And by you trying to beat the idea into my skull with your clenched fists that unchecked fracking is responsible in every way? And by me simultaneously taunting you with a winded (I'm 47 after all) rendition of "Sticks and stones may break my bones but meth can never hurt me!! (Nah nah na nah na!)."

And by me further telling you that being a citizen for responsible fracking pretty much means, for the time being, being a citizen for no fracking. (Until they figure out how to use Full Throttle as a drilling lubricant?)

What would us fighting in a parking lot do other than create some cheap theater for the other convenience store shoppers? We'd be one broken, wooden kitchen-chair-over-the-head away from being on *The Jerry Springer Show*.

Just before you catch me in the parking lot by my tax-and-spend liberal collar though, (and bear in mind that I shop at Goodwill before you damage my wardrobe) I'd start a straight jog down the road. I can run for four hours without stopping (or puking) so long as I have my iPod. Can you? Even with four cans of Full Throttle in you? Arggghhh!

Truth is, you and me?? We're probably very similar (except for the stealing hay, crystal meth, fracking, parking lot fights, NRA stroking, gambling and feeding da kids Twizzlers part). We're just a couple guys trying out our strong opinions in the court of public opinion here on the pages of the *BlueStone Press*.

Riddle me this: Half of the letters I receive here jam this paper for being too conservative. The other half jam it for being too liberal.

Half of the hay I put out gets stolen (thank YOU!). The other half gets paid for.

So I just wear my underwear inside out now. What else is there to do?

And oh—thanks for the invitation to swim in your pond. Super sweet and impossibly generous. (Is it heated? Cause I'm kinda a pussy about cold water. Otherwise, though, I got my Speedo on and am ready to go.)

And how's that scratch-off lottery thing working out for you??

Thanks for writing, and thanks for reading!

-Wally

PS: Might start raising chickens and putting eggs out on the stand so long as you promise to snag a few every now and again with your hay (my hay, that is) when no one's looking!!